MW00559442

THE RAVIN MARION, LOOKING NORTH ACROSS THE BATTLEFIELD OF THE REGIMENT'S THREE ATTACKS; ITS DEPTH MAY BE NOTED FROM THE PATH VAGUELY SEEN ALONG ITS BOTTOM.

FROM UPTON TO THE MEUSE

WITH THE
THREE HUNDRED AND
SEVENTH INFANTRY

A BRIEF HISTORY OF ITS LIFE AND OF THE PART
IT PLAYED IN THE GREAT WAR

BY

W. KERR RAINSFORD

CAPTAIN THREE HUNDRED AND SEVENTH INFANTRY

D. APPLETON AND COMPANY
NEW YORK   LONDON
1920

TO THE MEMORY OF ITS DEAD
AND AS A TRIBUTE TO ITS LIVING.
TO THEIR CHEERFUL ENDURANCE
UNDER EXHAUSTING PRIVATION,
AND TO THEIR COURAGE IN THE FACE OF DANGER

THIS BOOK IS DEDICATED

FOREWORD

The history of the 807th Infantry is the history of faithful service and devotion to duty of an organization which formed part of the 77th Division during the Great War. The name of the regiment is linked forever with the names of MERVAL, REVILLON, and LA PETITE MONTAGNE in the OISE-AISNE Offensive; it fought in the center of the ARGONNE FOREST, took the town of GRAND PRÉ and advanced triumphantly to the MEUSE in the course of the final operations which broke the enemy opposition. The example set by this organization is such as to inspire patriotism and devotion to duty whether in military life or in civil pursuits.

HEADQUARTERS 77TH DIVISION
Hotel Biltmore
New York City

ROBERT ALEXANDER
MAJOR GENERAL, U. S. A.
COMMANDING 77TH DIVISION

INTRODUCTION

Histories are too often builded upon the fallible memory of man, wherein the records of events are liable to be tinted with that exuberance which so often surrounds the fisherman's catch. In order that the splendid service which was rendered by the 807th Infantry, 77th Division of the National Army, in the great World War, might be perpetuated while the events were still fresh in memory, while official documents and pictures were available, and reconnaissance of battlefields could be made, this work was started in January, 1919, when the regiment was still in France and before the work could be influenced by that too easy divergence from facts which the narrator so soon weaves into his story in absolute credence.

. After very careful consideration of the necessary qualities and personality for a historian whose work could be accepted without question, I selected Capt. W. K. Rainsford, then commanding Company L, 807th Infantry, for the task. All official documents in the 807th Infantry and the 77th Division were made available to him, and leave was granted him for a reconnaissance of the terrain over which the regiment had fought.

Captain Rainsford was graduated from Harvard in 1904 and from the École des Beaux Arts, Paris, in 1911. During 1915–16 he served with the American Ambulance section attached to the French Army, and in this capacity participated with the French during the big German attack on Verdun in June, 1916. He attended the first Plattsburg Officers' Training Camp in 1917 and was commissioned a captain of infantry therefrom. In September, 1917, he was assigned to the 77th Division and placed in command of Company M, 807th Infantry. As commander of this company he went to France with his regiment and after training with the British Army took part in the defense of the Baccarat sector and the Oise-Aisne offensive, until wounded in front of Château Diable in August, 1918.

Returning from hospital in September he was placed in command of Company L, 807th Infantry, and was for the second time severely wounded in October, while leading his company in the first attempt to reach Major Charles W. Whittlesey's command, composed of parts of the 808th and 807th Infantry, which had been cut off and surrounded by the Germans in the Argonne Forest. In December Captain Rainsford was again returned from hospital to duty with his regiment.

This work is therefore commended to its readers as an official product from the pen, not of an onlooker but of a participant who endured every privation and hardship with the regiment; one who had watched the Great War from its beginning with the eye of a professional soldier, and who had served therein with the greatest valor and self-sacrifice from 1915 until the end.

Little can I express the great admiration, respect and affection I feel for every man of this splendid regiment, which I never commanded in battle but watched in every action, first while Chief of Staff of the 77th Division of the National Army to which it belonged, and then as commander of its companion regiment in the 154th Infantry Brigade, the 308th Infantry, during the last month of intense fighting in the Argonne.

The entire Division was drawn from what the military critics of the time assumed was the poorest fighting material in the United States, that greatest of all melting pots of humanity—New York City. Men unused to the sturdy activity of outdoor life; men who had had little chance for that physical development which enables them to endure great privation, fatigue and suffering; men who had no knowledge of woodcraft and the use of firearms, and in consequence were lacking in the principles of self-preservation and the confidence which comes from such knowledge. Yet these men, inducted into the service when their nation was in peril, after a brief period of training were thrown against the most perfectly trained and disciplined army the world has ever known. They fought their way to victory and never once gave ground to the enemy. Always enduring with perfect cheerfulness and courage every hardship and privation, responding at all times to their leaders, they accepted with equal tenacity of purpose and disregard of self the necessity for a frontal attack on the enemy's machine-gun nests or long sleepless nights and days, drenched to the skin and foodless, shivering with the cold, with no protection from the elements or the enemy's terrible weapons of destruction. A complaint was never heard, failure to obey was a thing unknown. Men who had lived in the glare of electric lights and had never known darkness fought their way night and day through fifteen miles of the most impenetrable mass of dense forest and underbrush, wire entanglements and trenches, that mind can conceive, in the Fôret d'Argonne.

No division suffered greater hardships, had greater losses during the time it was in line, nor was better disciplined and trained than this cosmopolitan division of New York City—the 77th, New York's Own.

If our nation is properly to protect its great wealth and future trade development, and more than all its homes and the lives of its people, no more forceful argument for the universal training of our young men can be presented than the history of this regiment and division. A brief period of intensive training made splendid officers from raw material, and nine months of similar training in service developed the army which whipped the Hun.

But let us not drift into the fallacy that there will always be buffer states between us and the enemy to protect us while this training is in progress. The deeds of this regiment exemplify what our splendid manhood can and will do for their country; what splendid patriotism comes from the crucible of American citizenship. Let us profit by past experience and in times of peace prepare for any eventuality, not by attempting to create a huge and expensive regular establishment but by training our young men in the use of arms, with that healthful, vigorous training which makes better men of them morally and physically, so that we will at all times be ready to safeguard our country against the encroachments and avarice of an enemy. When arbitration fails and we must throw down the gauntlet for the preservation of right, let us not send them forth incompletely trained and equipped, thus inviting an unnecessary waste of life, through a misconceived economy or that more charitable though equally fallacious belief of the pacifist, that wars are of the past. Preparedness is war's antitoxin. Had we been prepared in 1914 the *Lusitania* would never have been sunk.

J. R. R. HANNAY,
COLONEL U. S. ARMY
(FORMERLY COMMANDING 307th INFANTRY)

PREFACE

The following brief history was written for the most part during the latter months of the Regiment's stay in France, and was pieced together, in so far as the events recorded had not come under the writer's direct observation, from a number of sources. Such documents as the Regiment still held in its possession were carefully studied, but these were very insufficient and often inconclusive. They consisted largely of orders, which might afterward have been countermanded, or else simply never have been carried out as contemplated. They consisted also of reports which had been called for on specific subjects or actions; but these also would often have been written without adequate time for their preparation, and under stress of more pressing matters by officers greatly overtaxed. The battalion war diaries in General Headquarters at Chaumont were also studied. But there again the line or two devoted to the day's activity of a battalion was too meager a contribution to be greatly helpful; and when action had been serious and continuous it was often represented simply by a gap in the records.

The barest skeleton of the story could thus be built and the filling in of it was found to be best accomplished by continuously interviewing those who had taken part in its various phases. In this connection the reader may be struck by a slight but unintentional overemphasis of the battalion to which the writer belonged, and with the life-history of which he was more intimately familiar. There may also be an under-emphasis of any headquarters higher than that of battalion, which, rather than regiment, is the combat-unit of the modern army. But the effort has been consistent and very painstaking for truth of both fact and color; and the story herewith presented is primarily a true story. On that point the writer wishes to be emphatic.

The reader will find herein little of the colorful melodrama with which the public's taste has so largely been vitiated in the stories of war. As a case in point he will find no mention of bayonet-fighting. It is difficult to turn to a single magazine-illustration of fighting in the Argonne Forest wherein at least one of the American soldiers is not seen driving his bayonet through the body of a German machine-gunner, while the latter raises inadequately

protesting hands to the sky—and quite probably every American in the picture will be so
engaged. Yet, at the risk of deeply shocking
his public, the writer gives it as his careful
opinion that probably no German machine-
gun crew was ever bayoneted by Americans in
the Forest of Argonne. Although his regiment, perhaps more than any other, bore the
bitter brunt of fighting down the whole bloody
length of that forest, he yet thinks it improbable that any soldier of the regiment,
either there or elsewhere, ever used his bayonet
at all. It may have occurred, but if so it was
a rarity. Nor does this imply any slightest
lack on the part of the troops engaged—certainly not any lack of intelligence. The
bayonet became obsolete with the passing of
trench warfare. Place a group of men, armed
with machine-guns, magazine-rifles, and automatic pistols, free-footed in the woods, and try
hurdling the barbed-wire toward them with a
spear in your hand. You will infallibly be
mourned by your relatives—if they loved you
—and the machine-gun will still be in action.
In innumerable conversations with officers
from almost all the American combat-divisions
whom he met in hospitals, the writer has never
heard an authentic and first-hand account of
bayonet-fighting. It is altogether unworthy

of true courage and self-sacrifice that the story of it should be falsified to suit a supposedly popular taste.

The story herewith presented is then primarily true. In so far as it deals with the 307th Infantry alone it is known to be true; and in so far as it touches upon other organizations it is believed to be so—but not as the result of any special investigation. Since writing the chapter on the crossing of the Aire, for example, the writer has learned of some dispute between the 153rd Brigade and the 82nd Division as to the taking of St. Juvin. On this, or on similar subjects not directly germane to his narrative, he has made no great effort to investigate, and has not thought it worth while to qualify his reference to the taking of St. Juvin by the 153rd Brigade. The references made to other organizations are merely intended to give the story of the 307th its proper setting, and to suggest the relation of its movements to the scheme of larger events, rather than to define the movements of those organizations.

The sketches and photographs used to illustrate the text were made by the author,—the first when, as an ambulance driver with the French in 1916, he traversed in part the same region, and the latter when he revisited the battle-fields of the Vesle and Aisne in March, 1919—six months after they had been fought over. He greatly regrets that the subjects presented should not be of more obvious and general interest, and he made every effort, though unsuccessfully, to secure some that were.

Yet to himself the photographs are of deep interest, as were those few days of March on which they were taken. The return, as of a spirit escaped from purgatory, to that drear half-forgotten country—the battered villages, with their pitiable inhabitants creeping back to ruined homes; the broken woodlands with their trampled wreckage of equipment, still un-gathered, rotting slowly into the ground; the flooded marshes, where the river, choked with débris, backed and spread into stagnant pools; the bleak, scarred uplands, seen through a mist of rain and driving snow, where black flocks of rooks winged back and forth, or perched in hordes along the tangled wire; and from the hills, where the French engineers were setting off unexploded shells, the same heavy orchestra as of yore. It is a land accursed whose re-generation will be long in coming.

The two poems have both previously ap-peared in the *Outlook*. The first was written on February 21st, 1918, while spending a night alone as Officer of the Day in the 71st Regiment Armory in New York, where the 307th Infantry had left its arms under guard for the parade of Washington's Birthday. The officers of the Regiment had recently adopted for it the old Gaelic motto of the Irish Inniskillen Dragoons, "Faugh-a-Ballagh" ("Clear the Way"), and had agreed to carry blackthorn sticks as a regimental emblem. It was said that the Regiment would be known as the Blackthorn Regiment, although actually the name never clung very close. These verses were afterward read to Congress by the member from Michigan, and reprinted in the Congressional Record. The second was written in hospital, late during the fateful month of October, 1918, when it was becoming evident to those behind the lines that the final act of the great drama was about to be played.

Finally the writer thinks it well to say that, though largely written in France, this book was at the time of the mustering out of the Regiment on May 9, 1919, still in very fragmentary form, so that it was not read by any superior officer. Should there appear in its pages any passages seeming by implication to be critical, such criticism is that solely of the writer and of the brother officers with whom he has conferred, and does not in any way bear the indorsement of the greatly respected colonel or the general who have so generously prefaced it, but who have never had the opportunity to see its contents. Criticism is far from the purpose of this present volume, but in dealing very frankly with the facts, as seen on the Line, it may occasionally seem to be implied.

The writer was informed by the Regimental Adjutant, shortly before demobilization, that he had received notice of the Regiment being chosen from among the others of the Division for perpetuation in the Army of the United States. This, to become fact, would be conditional upon the proposed enlargement of the Regular Army to five hundred thousand, under which circumstances one regiment is to be selected from each of various divisions for perpetuation. The 77th Division, already distinguished as the first division of the Draft to be sent overseas, has been officially credited, in the report of Gen. Peyton C. March, Chief of Staff, with the greatest aggregate depth of territory gained from the enemy of any American Division in France—77.5 kilometers, or 9.14 per cent. of the entire advance of the American forces—there being twenty-seven divisions listed in all, and the 2nd Division coming next with 60 kilometers.

The 307th Infantry has been selected per-

PREFACE

manently to represent the Division, than which
no greater recognition of its service could well
be accorded it. This, then, is the story of the
Regiment, the purpose of which is truthfully
to portray some aspects of an epoch very memorable in the life of the nation.

W. K. RAINSFORD
Captain 307th Infantry

FAUGH-A-BALLAGH

There's a Blackthorn Regiment belongs to Uncle Sam,
  And it's heading out for trouble any day.
Be it France, or Greece, or Italy, it doesn't give a
    damn,
  Only start it on its road and Clear the Way!

Clear the Way before us when our marching orders
      come!
Can't you hear the fifes a-screaming and the throb-
      bing of the drum,
And the roar of marching feet
Down the crowded city street,
Past the avenues of faces? It's the long good-bye for
      some.
It's the price we gladly pay
To the Resurrection Day.
Let us pay it as we play it—Faugh-a-Ballagh! Clear
      the Way!

We've a debt that's due to England. We've a price to
      pay for France.
  We've a score with God Almighty we would pay.
We have talked and we have dallied while the others
      staked our chance.
  It is time we drew our cards—so Clear the Way!

FAUGH-A-BALLAGH

There's a length of battered trenches where the trees
     are torn and dead,
  With the reek of rotting horses in the air;
Where through blinding fog the shells come wailing
     blind overhead,
  And it's waiting for us now—over there.

Where the yellow mud is splattered from the craters
     in the snow,
  Where the dice of death are loaded—let us play.
We have pledged our word to Freedom,—and it's there
     that we would go,
  In the strength that Freedom gives us—Clear the
     Way!

Clear the way to No Man's Land, with bugles shrill
     and high;
Clear it to the lid of Hell, with flags against the sky.
Oh, clear the way to Kingdom Come, and give us glad
     good-bye.
We've a blow to strike for Freedom—Clear the Way!
                         W. K. R.

21ST FEBRUARY, 1916
  ARMORY 71ST N.G.N.Y.

CONTENTS

ILLUSTRATIONS

With the
THREE HUNDRED AND
SEVENTH INFANTRY

CHAPTER I

THE 307th Infantry, 154th Brigade, 77th Division, National Army, came into confused being at Camp Upton, Long Island, with the first increment of the draft from New York, in September, 1917. Its officers were of a high average of intelligence and natural ability, but their experience in war was for the most part limited to that gained at Plattsburg from the I.D.R., the F.S.R., and the imperishable Sergeant Hill; its enlisted personnel, for it was ordered that the drafted men should be so designated, was very largely from the East Side of the city, and contained every nationality that America has welcomed to her shores, but almost none who, on any pretext, had handled a rifle; its camp site was a recently cleared area of dust or mud, according to the weather,

1

gridironed by dirt roads, occupied in part by two-story wooden shacks but more largely by piles of lumber, and surrounded by, first, a zone of uprooted pine-stumps, then a space of charred pine-stumps in place, and finally by an endless sea of scrub-pine and autumn-tinted oak stretching down to the distant Sound. On Headquarters Hill alone a scattering growth of pines, which had escaped the ax, lent a remote suggestion of natural beauty to the scene. In dry weather walls of dust swept from end to end of the encampment, and in wet weather lakes inconveniently appeared. But the work of construction continued simultaneously with that of mobilization, and both achieved final, if imperfect, completion.

The Colonel and Lieutenant-Colonel were of the regular army at lower rank, a very few of the lieutenants had held non-commissioned rank in the regular service, and to each company was sent from the regular army one or two men as sergeants. Of these last a few did excellent service as drill sergeants; but on the whole the experiment was not successful, and

2

the greater number were returned to the regiments whence they came.

The company officers had expected to encounter difficulties in their appointed tasks, and they did so, but not as they had anticipated. The draft arrived in groups of from thirty to sixty or more, usually following behind a box-standard bearing the number of the Local Board, and in charge of a temporary leader, who submitted a list of their names and an armful of their appropriate papers. While the receiving officer, on the steps of his barracks, was ascertaining the innumerable discrepancies between the two, the draft stood about eyeing him with expectant curiosity, with friendly amusement, with critical displeasure, or with apathy, according to their nationality or mood—with any and every emotion save military respect. Then came the calling of the roll and further discrepancies. Certain men would answer with alacrity to each of three names called, or stand silent while their own was called as many times. As a typical instance, a man in "M" Company had answered "Here" at every formation for nearly a week before he was discovered to have been left at home on account of illness, and never to have reported at the camp. Another ghost was laid by the following dialogue:

"Morra, T."

"Here."

"Morra, R."

(From the same individual) "Here."

"Does your first name begin with a T. or an R.?"

"Yes, sir."

"Is your first name Rocco?"

"Yes, sir."

"What is your first name?"

"Tony."

And all in perfectly good faith.

They were at this stage known as "casuals," and after feeding them, one of the earliest duties was to interview each personally and ascertain his civilian occupation, probable capacity in it, and preference as to branch of service, although his statement as to the latter seemed but seldom to affect his ultimate fate.

Then came the fitting of uniforms. One set of all possible sizes was available for try-

4

ing on to each battalion, though not often to any of its companies; the consolidated requisitions were made out and submitted, and were filled, of necessity, piecemeal in the course of days or weeks; by which time the casuals had largely been sent to other organizations, and others, coming as casuals from elsewhere, had taken their place. These brought with them memoranda of their required sizes, or had lost them, as the case might be. It was the usual experience that the sizes noted were not the sizes required, that the sizes received were very possibly not the sizes requisitioned, and that the articles had probably been marked with the wrong sizes in the first instance. The men took the fit of their uniform seriously, as a soldier should, and a company commander's time was about equally distributed between those whose breeches offended their better judgment, those whose broken arches prevented their marching, those who (through interpreters) were unnaturalized Russians and did not belong in the draft at all, and, commonest ailment, those whose perishing family required their immediate presence at home.

5

The evil, probably unavoidable in any army, of detailing officers away from their companies to special duty, had already made itself felt, and at this time a very typical company of the regiment had three hundred and eighty-five recruits to feed, clothe, discipline, control, and train, a six-inch litter of papers on the table of the otherwise unfurnished orderly-room, each calling for immediate compliance or report, and three officers present for duty. General Sherman only half expressed himself.

The organization of the rifle companies was made difficult by the very constant transfer of men to specialist groups, to other branches of the service, or to other training camps. If a recruit was quick and intelligent he was probably found to be also an electrician, and was transferred to the signal platoon, or a chauffeur, and went to the motor transport, or else he looked promising as a machine-gunner, accountant, or one-pound cannoneer, and also disappeared. Camp Gordon, strangely in need of men, offered a certain safety-valve, and the man whose face seemed irreconcilable with a steel helmet, whose name on the roll-call consisted only of consonants, or who had cast his rice pudding in the mess-sergeant's face often completed his training there—on the pretext that all is fair in war.

The training of the companies was made difficult by the lateness of the season and the lack of any adequate drill-ground or gymnasium. As the mud became more universal and deeper the few macadamized roads, notably Fifth Avenue, became attractive for the drilling of squads and for close order march; but the consequent interference with traffic led to this being strictly prohibited. Troops were forbidden to move at any time in greater frontage than column of twos upon the hard roads, or to cross them except by infiltration; this, with the unauthorized taking of loose building-material—defined to include any piece of lumber greater than two inches square or two feet in length—for the purpose of interior improvements or firewood, formed a constant Sword of Damocles over the head of any company commander whose three hundred and eighty recruits were at any time out of his sight.

7

Another increment of the draft was received in December and again in February, each followed by its period of wholesale transfers; so that, even as late as the latter month, a stranger in civilian clothes who appeared unannounced in the orderly-room, with his hat on his head, to offer the company commander a red apple, might still be a member of his command. But by this time the good material was coming to the fore. Corporals and sergeants had been found who could take hold of their men, drill them, and enforce regulations; and there never was any apparent unwillingness on the part of the enlisted men to serve, nor conscious wish to defy authority.

It was wonderful how willingly they seemed to prepare for a war of which so many could not know the meaning. Three thousand miles across the sea, what could it mean to the late worker in the East-side sweat-shop that Messine Ridge was retaken by the Germans? And yet they were ready to prepare to take their place upon that distant line. There were a few conscientious objectors, of whom at least some were evidently sincere, letter-perfect in their Bible texts and unwilling to shed the blood of others; there were a very few who, with or without the sanction of Biblical precedent, were frankly unwilling to shed their own; there were also some of German parentage who were excusably unwilling to face their relatives with a rifle. These were the rare exceptions, yet in passing let the methods be noted by which it was directed that they should be dealt with—for these methods were the same as those which saved the lives of numbers of enemy agents in the land, at the cost of the lives of innumerable citizens. A conscientious objector of another regiment had definitely and finally refused to put on his uniform when so ordered by his company, battalion, and regimental commanders, with the somewhat startling result that officers were notified that "they would be held responsible not to place themselves in the position of issuing a direct order to their men." With other types of men the position might well have become impossible; but it was not so. And oh, the pathos of those poor Italians, and Slavs, and Jews—Americans all—who came to their company commanders with the letters from their sick wives, uncared for, and often about to be ejected from their pitiful homes, letters uncomplaining and only asking when the husband could return for a little while; and the men, on their part, only asking what provision could be made for their women-folk while they were away, seldom asking for the exemption which they should have had by right, but of which they had been defrauded by some Local Board, more concerned over the safety of its native sons than over the rights of its foreign-born residents. They were lovable men, probably because nearly all men become lovable when the relations between them are right, and are long continued.

The nearness of New York, however, while a convenience to the individual, was a decidedly adverse factor to discipline and control; and the men, except those from up-State, never quite cut loose from the city nor gave themselves unreservedly to the military life. The difficulty of A.W.O.L. (absence without leave) was pronounced throughout the entire period at Camp Upton, and that of drunkenness, while not acute, was always to be reckoned with.

There was very little training with special arms at this time. The rifle range was used as often as the weather permitted, and, though this was not begun until winter had set in, the men showed decided aptitude for the work. Bayonet drill was frequent, although complicated by two or three different schools of technique, to which selected lieutenants or N. C. O.'s (non-commissioned officers) were sent for instruction, and which usually concluded their course with a warning that, in view of a more recent method having been ordered since the opening of the course, the methods of instruction just taught should not be practiced with the troops. The throwing of dummy grenades was practiced as taught by a French lieutenant, but live hand-grenades or rifle-grenades were never available. The instruction with automatic rifles did not go beyond that of the mechanism of the Lewis Gun and chauchat for two N. C. O.'s and a lieutenant from each company, with a single day's firing on the range. The guns were never available for the training of squads in the companies. The open-order formations of the English and French, as gleaned from pamphlets, were grafted onto the American regulations more or less according to the theory or understanding of the individual company commander, and the troops were drilled in them in the snowy stump-fields.

The late increments of recruits, while distracting and disorganizing, had at least the advantage of giving the older men a pride in their seniority and more confidence in their authority. The number of officers had been increased, both from the later Plattsburg camp and from Camp Mills, to an average of nearly ten per company; amusement halls had been constructed; little pine and cedar trees had been planted about a number of the barracks; the train journey to and from the city had been reduced from six or eight hours to an average of two—and the cars were occasionally heated—and by midwinter life was moving upon ordered ways. It was a rather severe winter, but, except for the lack of facilities for indoor exercise and training, brought no real hardships; the barracks were fairly well-heated, for, in spite of the coal famine in the civilian world, coal was never lacking at camp, and, in the light of after experience, the quantity and quality of the food-ration was extraordinary.

One special feature of the training provoked a real, if transitory, thrill; this was the gas-chamber. The men had been told about gas, about the gas that burned out your lungs, the gas that blistered off your skin, the gas that blinded your eyes, that made you vomit, and that made you sneeze; they had been told what to do about each; they had been warned and lectured to by English and French experts with experience, and by American experts without it; they had been practiced to a seven-second adjustment of gas-masks; they had been marched in gas-masks, and had played games in them. And then on the outer confines of camp appeared the gas-chamber; and, after a final inspection of masks for pin-pricks, and after a sort of final benediction, one platoon at a time—while the others sat upon the neighboring slopes singing a funeral march—one platoon at a time, they filed into, and were sealed within, the gas-chamber. There was no slightest actual danger, and yet it was interesting. Even so early came a slight forewarning of that coming readjustment of values, when the too-often drunken ne'er-do-well and the recognized public nuisance should come to their own. Even so early one glimpsed ahead to the man who would push forward laughing into the unknown; or to him who, when his company drew back from its latest Golgotha, might be found with a scarlet brassard about his arm, doing police-duty at a cross-road, and uneager to tell how he got there.

To one who spent Christmas at the Camp—and by far the greater number were able to go home—that day forms one of its pleasantest memories. There were a scattered few, disconsolate in the empty barracks, wishing they too were at home, or looking apathetically out on the fine rain that gathered in icicles along the eaves. And then volunteers were called for to bring in pine branches and trailing vines to decorate the mess-halls. They all volunteered. Probably no one can quite resist the cheering influence of gathering and

14

decorating with Christmas greens; and the rain didn't matter, for it never does except to the homeless; and the Red Cross sent to every one in camp a package prettily tied with ribbons, enclosing things to eat or smoke, and things to play with or use, and a card of Christmas greeting from some girl, unknown and therefore lovely; and the small numbers led to a new intimacy, and the loneliness of the barracks turned to a cozy seclusion; and Christmas found its way again into the heart.

On a snowy twenty-second of February the Division paraded through New York before one of the largest crowds the city had ever gathered, and was greeted with very considerable enthusiasm. Camp Upton was proud of what it had produced, only regretting that it had to court-martial so many of its members immediately thereafter for lack of a proper sense of when the festivities were over. This event being passed, the mind of the camp began seriously to concentrate on the coming departure for overseas, and it is not too much to say that, until after that departure, the regiment never really found itself. In probably every company one or two N. C. O.'s had shown that absolute reliance could be placed upon them as leaders of their men; for a much larger number it was confidently hoped that under war-time conditions their power to command would develop; but the great mass of men still constituted an ununified, unknown, and very insufficiently trained quantity, who had never yet learned to take themselves seriously as soldiers, though giving no evidence of unwillingness to serve. A resifting of officers now took place to eliminate the supernumeraries, and further effort was made, though with very partial success, to get rid of the men known to be physically or mentally incompetent.

The question of equipment assumed a leading rôle. There were lectures and bulletins to officers on the subject of their appropriate and necessary equipment—a selection of articles seeming, in the light of after experience, rather extraordinary. Equipment C for the troops was eventually defined, and the Gordian tangle of property responsibility, brought about by the wholesale and simultaneous equipment and

16

transfer of masses of men without any authorized or recognized forms for receipt, which had hung broodingly in the background for months, was finally severed, as Gordian tangles only can be. Some notes from a diary, kept at this time by the author, will perhaps best picture the beginning of April.

"April 4th.—Equipment C blocks the horizon, together with the number of packing cases to be allowed, and where they are to come from. Some of the companies have over thirty. We haven't; but the First Sergeant promises to produce an average of two or three per night. Our fifteen square-headed shovels have dwindled to twelve, though we have four or five round-headed ones, apparently of no use for digging trenches. All efforts to exchange them through regular channels having failed, the First Sergeant is sending out men in couples this evening, with one shovel per couple, to quarrel in the vicinity of distant coalbins, and try to change the shape of their heads. (Later.) We have fifteen square-headed shovels.

"April 5th.—We are to be recruited to full strength and packed to-day. Have received 165 new men off and on in the past month; 240 now on the Morning Report; the packing cases

are being held open till we know how many
we take and whom. At 10 A. M. got in seven
recruits, and at 10 P. M. eleven more—making
us over strength. The mechanics worked till
midnight last night packing up, and till noon
unpacking. The A.W.O.L.'s, absent sick, and
venereals transferred out about 10:30 P. M.
Formed the company after supper and stacked
arms and packs in company street, forming
again on stacks at 11 P. M. and again at 8
A. M. Policing continuous and apparently
hopeless. Every time I walked round the barracks I found a new pile of decaying quilts
and underclothes stacked on the ash-stand.
Nash has had burning and burying details going continuously. When the last fire had been
extinguished and the last shovel returned—at
8 A. M. formation—I found the store-room
of the Annex half-filled with straw and civilian
clothes. One rather hectic detail is resorting
and packing and marking the barrack bags of
those transferred out for those transferred in.
The boxes left at 11:45 P. M. to catch a twelve
o'clock train. Night very cold—a few of the
men drunk, but all apparently here.

"April 6th.—Marched out under arms and
packs at 4:15 A. M. All squads reported full,
all material shipped or turned in and credited,

and all paper work complete—rather incredible. Night turning warmer with a dying moon in the east—a silent march through a silent, deserted camp, bringing unexpected regrets of farewell.

"(Later.) A cloudless morning. Got into Long Island City about 7 A. M. and ferried around Battery Park to the White Star docks. Scattered cheering from the other ferries we passed and from a small crowd gathered along the Battery. Our ship—the *Justicia*—looks huge, and the officers' quarters as princely as those of the men look crowded and poor.

"April 7th.—Got under way about 7:30 A. M. I was too busy below to wave a farewell to the city but there was no send-off. The men are arranged with the utmost confusion—squads, platoons, companies, and even regiments—for we carry one battalion of the 308th—all rather hopelessly mingled and so assigned to places. My fourth platoon is in four different parts of the ship, with the Friday night recruits mostly in first-class cabins, while the balance of the company is herded in hammocks, that almost overlap, four decks below. Some, having no assignments to quarters or mess, are sleeping on tables and begging food, my mess-sergeant among them. No company officers were allowed on board until after the men were placed by the shipping authorities, and the men were loaded simultaneously by three gangways. Re-arrangement has to be surreptitious as it is forbidden by the ship's officer. Port-holes are painted black, fixed shut, and covered on the inside with zinc shields—which means we can have lights. No one on deck after 8 P. M.

"April 8th.—We got the men's quarters policed and scrubbed; and with the hammocks stowed they do look livable. Then we stood for some hours on boat drill. We are told that there is ample accommodation for all in case of accident, but I believe that the swimmers holding to the edge of the rafts are included among those accommodated. That would be poor at this season of the year, and there certainly are not enough boats. Life preservers are never to be left out of reach—a sort of fore-warning of gas-masks.

"We sighted Nova Scotia about 5 P.M. and passed the outer lighthouse of Halifax at sunset, anchoring far up in the inner harbor.

"April 9th.—A thin skim of glare ice over all the harbor, reflecting in sunshine the screaming flocks of gulls; hoar-frost along the

20

rails, and snow over the black, spruce-clad shores. The ocean and city are completely hidden by infolding hills. Boats were lowered at boat-drill and rowed about through the thin ice. The *Lapland* came in behind us, and a transport of Australians is anchored ahead. We weighed anchor about 5 P.M. and pulled out in long succession through the narrow channel—eight transports in column. Women and children gathered in groups along the shore holding out the Stars and Stripes to us; it seemed, too, to fly from the window of every cottage; the crews of the British ships and U. S. men-of-war lined their rails to cheer us as we passed, their bands playing with their whole souls. It was everything we had wanted and missed at New York, and one felt the tingling grip of brotherhood in the great world struggle on which we were launched. 'God Save the King,' 'The Star-Spangled Banner,' 'The Marseillaise,' and 'The Girl I Left Behind Me'—high resolve and dear regret, the warm throb of blood and the grip of cold steel; it was war and the long good-by at last. God grant that we do our part. The spires and roofs of Halifax lifted flat and purple against the yellow twilight under an arch of rosy cloud; then the ruins of the lower city swept and crumpled like a village in France; on our port the wreck of the Belgian Relief Ship, half-submerged, the sunset-gilded spruce woods and sandy islands, the quaint old white lighthouse, and the open sea."

CHAPTER II

THE convoy sailed for the most part in double line under escort of the cruiser *St. Louis*. Little occurred beyond the usual rumors of a sortie by the German fleet—most of whom were supposed to have gotten through— or some sudden semaphoring from ship to ship and activity on the part of the *St. Louis*, later explained by the presence of a whale.

On the evening of the seventeenth an escort of seven British destroyers appeared, ducking and dodging through the spume like a school of porpoises, and at dusk of the nineteenth the *Justicia* was docked at Liverpool. The troops were disembarked between ten and eleven P.M., and, looking their last on the great ship which loomed above, incredibly vast in the smoky moonlight, were placed directly upon train for Dover. The journey was bitterly cold, and impressions of England were only

28

cheered by the sight of an unusually pretty girl
serving coffee during a halt at Rugby about
three A.M., and by a clear sunrise over a country white with hoar-frost and cherry-blossoms.
Arriving at Dover about eight A.M. the troops
were marched under packs to what appeared
to be the summit of the highest hill in the
neighborhood for breakfast, and then immediately back to the steamer. Nobody liked
England; but the Channel presented a picture
of her grip of the seas—wreathed in the smoke
of innumerable destroyers, above which hov-
ered aeroplanes and dirigibles on watch, and
somewhere the distant firing of guns.

Reaching Calais in the early afternoon of
April 20, the battalions were marched to different Rest Camps and billeted, rather crowd-
edly, in tents sunk a few feet under ground
for protection from aerobombs. The baptism
of fire, though very mild, was immediate.
Shortly before midnight the siren wailed out
its alarm over camp; then came the discharge
of guns, the soaring scream of projectiles, the
occasional soft "thut" of a bullet falling into
the sand, and the shock of explosives beyond

the canal in the city. From somewhere over-head amid the weaving and crossing search-lights, and the sparkling flash of shrapnel, could be heard the recurrent whirr of German motors—later so familiar a sound—but only the city of Calais paid whatever price was to pay.

Two days were spent in fitting and drawing gas-masks, steel helmets, and ammunition, and exchanging rifles for the British arm; and at noon of the twenty-third, leaving a few sick behind, the troops were marched to the station at Calais and carried by train some twenty kilometers to Audriq. From this point the battalions were marched to their different training areas—the First at Zouafque, the Second at Nordasque, the Third at Louches, and Regimental Headquarters at Tournehem. The marches were not long, varying from ten to fourteen kilometers, but, as had been an-ticipated, the packs proved too heavy for all except the strong men. They carried at this time two blankets, shelter-half with pole and pins, overcoat, slicker, extra boots and under-clothes, two days' rations, rifle, bayonet, can-

25

teen, and 150 rounds of ammunition, forming a pack which came down to the knees of the smaller men. It was a punishing march, accentuated in the case of the Third Battalion by the guide losing the way, and the beauties of spring in the French lanes were apparent to few accept those on horseback.

In these areas the battalions stayed for three weeks, making their first acquaintance with French villages and billets, with their distant picturesque charm and their nearby atmosphere of all-pervading manure heaps. Lieutenants and N. C. O.'s from every company were sent to specialist schools, principally for the Lewis Gun; the captains were sent on three- or four-day visits to the British front line south of Arras—a dreary stretch of half-dug trenches in the mud, rambling through shattered hamlets and golden fields of dandelions, where the sniper fired across six or eight hundred yards of rusted wire—mostly German—and life was made equally unhappy by the enemy's minenwerfers and one's own six-inch "hows."

The writer was assigned to a part of the

line held by the First Royal Berkshires and then taken over by the K. R. R.; and he was privileged to accompany a captain of the latter on his initial inspection of the front. It was a night of gusty rain and of utter darkness, but the British captain, a veteran of the South African War, treated it as though it were a pleasant afternoon, and No Man's Land as though it were his own front garden. He took up a pick helve, which he carried in lieu of a walking stick, and the two started forth. There was little difficulty in scaling the front parapet—one merely stepped out of it—but soon afterwards one's impressions became confused. They crossed belts of wire as though it had been an obstacle race; they skirted invisible shell craters almost on the run; they leaped chasm-like trenches on faith that there was a farther side; occasionally they stopped to listen, but for the most part they simply traveled, and at a speed seeming quite beyond reason. After perhaps an hour and a half there were voices; and, just as the writer was preparing to sell his life dearly, they dove through a blanket into the covered shelter from

which they had first started, and the English
captain began at once issuing minute instructions for the wiring of empty gaps in the line,
for the improvement of certain lengths of
trench, and for the relocation of some of his
Lewis guns.

This was a time of anxious waiting for all
in France. Two great German blows had
already been delivered that spring, and from
the force of their impact the British army had
reeled back defeated and all but crushed. The
face of the war, brightening greatly during the
last two years, had in a month become horribly
changed. The future seemed more than doubtful; it seemed desperate. France had little
left to bring to a losing war, and England, un-
conquerable England, awaited the next blow
with a grimness akin to despair, and her mind
already prepared for a peace which should
bring no victory. This at least was the spirit
encountered among the British troops, of
whom a captain, wearing the ribbons of the
M. C. and D. S. O., with whom the present
writer had become intimate, said to him one
day, as though encouragingly: "Now that you

Americans have come over I feel sure, sure, that you'll find we'll stick it out. Otherwise, I think we would have patched up some sort of a peace this spring, but now I'm *sure* that we'll carry on some way."

And the National Army had never dreamed it. Their only thought had been that they might not be in time to share the victory with their Allies. But now they learned to listen to the dull orchestra of the guns at night, and to try to guess at their message. Rumor, unofficial but persistent, had said that when next the Germans struck all troops, trained or untrained, were to be flung in their path—for all would likely be needed.

Captain Illingworth, an English officer of the 16th Sherwood Foresters, with his staff of specialist N. C. O.'s, was assigned temporarily to the regiment to assist in the instruction of the troops; and he rendered in this a very real service, though, as always heretofore, the lack of adequate training ground was keenly felt, and the French in this region were far from generous in making such available. Yet thirty-yard rifle-ranges with reduced targets were improvised, where the men learned the use of their new weapons; and the Lewis Gun teams, four to each platoon, picked from the best material, took hold of their work with genuine enthusiasm, evincing the first real *esprit de corps* to be developed.

On May fourteenth, after three weeks of almost daily rain, the battalions marched again to Audriq, where they took train to Mondicourt, some 25 kilometers southwest of Arras. Here they were to be brigaded for training, and it was thought also for combat, with different battalions of Manchester and East Lancashire troops, of the Forty-second British Division. The First battalion at Couin, the Second at Henu, and the Third with Regimental Headquarters at Pas, were all within a radius of three kilometers. It was an impressive arrival, the short march from Mondicourt, before dawn on the fifteenth, through the sleeping, starlit village, with the nearer sound of the guns along the front, the climbing white caterpillar-lights, and, somewhere in the darkness ahead, a British band playing the troops magnificently in. They know how to use their music, the British, and it seemed strange that the regiment should leave America in the silence of the plague-stricken, to be escorted into the forward area with a brass band.

The three weeks here spent were probably the pleasantest in the army experience of any, either theretofore or thereafter. The country was beautiful, the weather immaculate, the training systematic and efficient. Save for the infrequent passage or seemingly unaimed arrival of a shell in the wheatfields, or the more frequent and important shortage in rations, there was little to mar the tranquillity of the summer days. The troops were quartered in large conical or small shelter-tents, as the case might be, along the edge of the splendid beech-woods, and, if only they could have learned to like the British ration, British shoes, and British Tommy, might have been perfectly happy. But the first was too short, the second too flat, and the trouble with the last rather difficult to determine. Unfortunately the American soldier, probably harking back to the injurious history books of school-days, decided to hate him; yet the feeling does not seem to have been reciprocal, and nothing could have exceeded the hospitality, courtesy, and welcoming, painstaking kindliness of the British officers.

There were dinners given, principally by the East Lancashires, frequent and astonishingly elaborate banquets, with delicious food and excellent wines, with music and song and story; and the British officers came riding in on their splendid, well-groomed horses, with sparkling equipment; and the American officers joined them upon less striking steeds, with patched saddles borrowed from some muleteer, and strips of rusty leather knotted into the length of reins; and they gathered together under the leafy beech-wood, carefree, or forgetful of care, while behind the sound of the singing, and the laughter, and the music, there hung, like a curtain across the distance, the steady thunder of the guns. Their stories never were of the war, nor did their songs refer to it.

> Now I, friend, drink to thee, friend,
>   As my friend drank to me,
> And as my friend charged me, friend,
>   So I, friend, charge thee.

WITH THE BRITISH

That thou, friend, drink to thy friend,
 As my friend drank to me,
And the more we drink together
 The merrier we'll be.

(Chorus, all together)

And the more we drink together
The merrier we'll be.

Brave, gallant gentlemen, their division was
heavily hit before the end of summer, and often
one wonders how many are still left of that gay
gathering.

The British Tommies gave open-air vaude-
ville performances in costume every week, at
which all American troops were always made
welcome; and when one day an American
Company established a new record of rifle-fire
on the bullet and bayonet course, the British
Sergeant-Major in charge of the course spread
the news with an enthusiasm and pride far beyond what he would have felt for a similar
achievement by his own men. The writer cap-
tained a battalion rifle-team to victory against
the team of a British battalion. The opposing
scores were very close, the Americans winning
by a narrow margin because two of their op-

ponents had done very poorly. They were heartily congratulated on their victory and no whisper of protest was heard. Not till afterward, and quite by accident, did the writer discover that when, at the request of the British Major, he had given the signal for the British team to commence firing—and the match was solely one of rapid fire—these two members of the team had been waiting for a preliminary order to load their magazines. Rather than interrupt an American officer, unfamiliar with their technique, or insist upon an even break, they had started on a competition in rapid fire with empty magazines, and cheerfully accepted the resultant defeat; and though every member of their team knew it, none had mentioned it.

At an American inter-company Sunday baseball game, Major-General Sully-Flood, a splendid type of British officer and gentleman, appeared as a very interested spectator, and at the conclusion of the game expressed a wish to take a turn at the bat. The American pitcher, a lean, loose-jointed Yankee, gave him a swift but straight ball, and the General knocked out something like a home-run. It was almost as good as an Allied victory.

On June sixth, and most regrettably just as these British units were about to return to the line in expectation of taking with them the battalions of the 307th, with whom they had more than equally divided their limited training grounds, all British equipment was ordered turned in, including rifles and the now beloved Lewis Guns, and the regiment marched west. The suddenness of this change at the moment of coming action was mortifying in the extreme, for it seemed almost like desertion in the face of the enemy. There might well have been a little jeering from the British, but there was none. Instead, to their honor be it said, a British band, hurriedly assembled, played them out upon their way; and with generous courtesy Major-General Sully-Flood stood at a cross-roads to salute and shake hands with the officers as they passed, and to wish them the best of luck. Their true sporting spirit taught the British how they themselves would have felt under like circumstances; with instinctive generosity they attributed a like view-

point to their friends, and one loved them for
it.

A four-day march was made to the entraining points at Longpré and Saint Remy, the
First Battalion halting at Gezaincourt, Berna-
ville, and Ailly-le-Haut-Clocher, the Second
at Longueville, Vacquerie, and Famechon, and
the Third at Candas, Berneuil, and Ailly-le-
Haut-Clocher. The first day's march only
was severe, some twenty-four kilometers, at
the end of which rifles and ammunition were
issued from trucks. The men's packs had been
reduced by one blanket, and it had been possible to get rid of the worst of the flat-footed
to special duty, so the march was not unpleas-
ant, and speculation was rife as to whither it
was leading. The wide valley of the Somme,
with its intricate maze of canals and lagoons
glittering in sunshine through the foliage of
innumerable lines of poplars, was a picture to
cherish.

The journey by train led west and south,
skirting Paris, then southeast to the Moselle,
where the regiment was detrained at Chatel
and Thaon on the night of June eleventh.

Save for the cold of the nights and the inevitable discomfort of cattle-cars, it was a memorable journey. The civilian population of every town flocked to windows and gardens to wave and cheer to "les Americains"; at every halt the loveliest in the land seemed to have been gathered to give out coffee and flowers along the station platforms; and at one momentary stop outside a tunnel a particularly sweet-looking French girl was found, by chance or otherwise, picking flowers beside the track. Having been kissed by one soldier, she continued generously along the length of the train, showing little or no favoritism, and, as the train moved on through the tunnel, her figure, in black silhouette against the diminishing arch of sunshine, kissing her hand again and again into the darkness, left a picture such as is good for fighting men to carry with them.

Detraining toward midnight, the battalions moved, the First to Longchamps and Girecourt, the Second to Bult, the Third to Sercœur and Dompierre, and Regimental Headquarters to Padoux. To show the contrast in hospitality of the people in this region to that accorded the troops in the north, a letter written at this time is worth quoting in part:

"Being mounted, I rode ahead through the darkness two or three miles to Vaxoncourt, where my company and another were to spend the rest of the night, for it seemed unlikely that any arrangements had been made for billeting the men. The village, on a little rocky hill surrounded by streams, was sound asleep, and I rode through its silent streets looking in vain for any light. Then, knocking with my whip at a shutter, I was told by a surprised and sleepy voice where the mayor lived, and pounded also at his shutter. The mayor slept well, but finally thrust out a nightcapped head to ask what was the matter. I told him that five hundred American troops were coming to billet in his village, but he said it was not possible that such a thing should happen, for it was after one o'clock. I explained that nevertheless I had only distanced them by the gait of my horse, and wanted him to help me arrange billets for them. He retired muttering, more dazedly than in ill-humor, and soon appeared in ulster and wooden sabots with a lantern. We went through the village, waking every one with the good news that the Americans were coming, till we had something like a full town-meeting gathered with lanterns in the public square. They treated it rather like a fête, every one lending a hand, pulling out wagons from the barns, setting ladders to the lofts, making up beds for the officers, and standing with lanterns at their doorways to welcome their allotment; so that when the column arrived, about half an hour behind me, they were marched straight to billets without a pause. I got a splendid room overlooking the meadows and orchards at the edge of town, where, in the morning, a beaming old woman brought me in a great bowl of hot milk and coffee, fresh bread, and a precious little dish of sugar—staunchly refusing to be paid for it. We left at noon the same day, all the inhabitants who were not working in the fields coming to wave us good-by and offer flowers.

"At Dompierre, where we arrived that afternoon, the feeling seemed to be just the same, though, on account of an epidemic of mumps in the village, we had the men pitch shelter-halves in the flat meadows along the stream. I spent the next morning riding about looking for drill-grounds, as we expected to be here a week, and then called on the mayor. I told him that in order to beat the Boche the men

had to be drilled and trained, and that the only
available ground seemed to be the recently har-
vested hay-meadows along the bottom of the
valley, though this would rather interfere with
their growing a second crop. He said they
were community meadows, and if I thought
them necessary for drilling the troops that was
probably a better use to put them to than
growing hay; after all, we were at war, and
the village did not want to be paid for them.
We had him and the *curé* and the town *gref-
fier* to dinner a few nights later, and it was
delightful to see them, with a glass of cham-
pagne in one hand and a slice of white American bread, which they insisted was *gateau,* in
the other, beaming at us as they tried to beat
time and join in our songs."

CHAPTER III

On June seventeenth, the First Battalion moved to the ruined hamlet of Mesnil, the high-water mark of German invasion in September, 1914, and thence, the next evening, to Vacqueville, a dirty and inhospitable little village close behind the rather ill-defined Line of Resistance. On the twentieth, Battalion Headquarters moved up to St. Maurice, with companies D and A on the front and support of the right sector at Neuviller, and companies C and B on the left in Grand Bois, relieving the forward elements of the Forty-second Division on the line during the night of the twenty-first. The Third Battalion moved on the eighteenth to the meadows outside Rambervillers, and the next evening through the town, against the turbulent counter-current of the Forty-second's Alabamans, a splendid-looking

41

lot of men, who appeared only by chance to be wearing uniforms.

With darkness came rain, at first a few large drops and then a roaring cloudburst. The evening had started fair and the raincoats were stowed inside the packs, where they alone remained dry. Somewhere in the drenching darkness ahead was a convoy of motor ambulances, traveling at the unexhausting rate of two miles an hour, and halting every fifteen or twenty minutes for repairs. Then the rain ceased and moonlight flooded the dark sprucewood, lighting mysterious vistas in its wet and misty depths. Through the gaunt ruins and moon-blanched streets of Mesnil the black column wound its way, looking beneath its gleaming steel like some invading host of old, but feeling less romantic than tired and wet. Toward midnight it reached Deneuvre on the hilltop overlooking Baccarat and billeted amid its crooked alleys in barns already crowded with troops who were supposed to have left.

The day following the troops moved across the Meurthe to the Haxo Barracks of Baccarat for another week of training, including the

first firing with the new rifles and recently issued chauchat guns, and the first general use
of rifle and live hand-grenades. The initial
nervousness of most in handling the latter, and
their evident desire to get rid of them, once
the detonator had been fired, in almost any
direction, was ample proof of the value of this
opportunity—without which, however, the
First Battalion had entered the line. On the
twenty-second, the Second Battalion took station on the Line of Resistance at Vacqueville,
where Regimental Headquarters had also been
located, and with the Supply Company at
Creviller the regiment had established itself
in its new sector.

The battalion at Haxo Barracks was for
rest and training; that at Vacqueville and Les
Carrieres for a perfunctory manning of the
Line of Resistance with half-companies, while
the rest could practice their chauchats and live
grenades in the nearby quarry; and the forward Battalion held two companies on the outpost line and two on the Line of Support,
which was in fact a line of resistance, that in
front of Vacqueville not yet having been dug.

The region about and behind the front was of vast woodlands alternating with open and dusty meadows. In places the woods had been blown to pieces with artillery fire, and in places the meadows were pitted with craters of sun-cracked clay. One particular stretch of open marsh, near some abandoned artillery emplace-ments on the Line of Resistance, had been churned up into something like the surface of a sponge, and still, on misty nights, reeked with the sickish acid smell of gas. The white dusty roads were lined with dilapidated fes-toons of burlap, or screens of wilted and dust-covered rushes—to shelter from observation such traffic as must pass. Little half-ruined vil-lages of roofless walls and tumbled masonry, like empty sea shells upon some desolate coast, lined the high-water mark of early invasion—and in the center of each rose the skeleton of some beautiful old church, its tower pierced with shell-holes and its entrance blocked by the fallen chimes.

The line was throughout jointly held with the French and under their command, one pla-toon of French being usually interlarded with

THE ENTRANCE BLOCKED BY THE FALLEN CHIMES

two of Americans. The intention was for the practical instruction of inexperienced troops in trench-life and patrolling, the sector being notoriously a quiet one—in fact the opposing lines were substantially as determined in the first winter of the war. But while the French, especially the company officers, did their very best to produce coöperation, the system was not regarded as successful by most on the American side. Extremely few of the officers and practically none of the enlisted men could speak each other's language, making whispered consultations in No Man's Land somewhat unfruitful of result; the orders for the defence of the sector were written in French and did not obtain translation until Major Jay, of the Second Battalion, so translated them during his tenure of the front; and the habit of the French outposts of firing on principle, broadcast through the night, got on the unseasoned American nerves, without mentioning the resultant danger to friendly patrols who were trying to win home.

At dawn of June twenty-fourth the regiment and the brigade first came to hand-grips

with the German, with results largely in favor
of the latter. Neuviller, a tiny ruined village

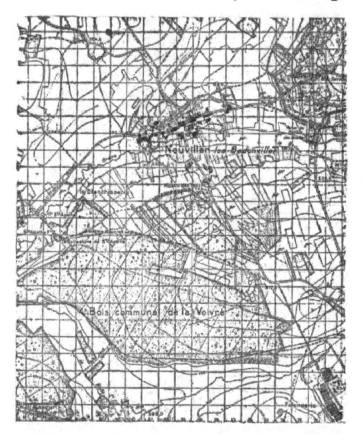

on an isolated hill, that must once have been
a very pleasant little spot, and is still, though
more grimly, picturesque, with its loopholed
cobblestone barricades, stood out as a danger-

46

ous salient from the French lines. The road
to it from St. Maurice was still intact, but
counted as No Man's Land; and its garrison
of two American platoons and one French had
only a single communicating trench, some three
hundred yards long, connecting it across the
marsh, for retreat or reënforcement, with their
supporting troops at the Moulin des Tocs and
Buisson, though at this time the support company was also forward in the Bois de la Voivre.
The defences of the village were an extensive
and intricate system of largely abandoned
trenches, whose field-of-fire, in so far as it had
ever existed, was in great measure obscured
by overgrowing bushes. There were also dugouts, which have no proper place on an outpost line, and all indications pointed to its having been originally laid out for a purpose quite
different from that for which it was now being
used. Its present garrison was too weak for
effective defense and too large for speedy withdrawal; the general orders of the Americans
were clear about holding any part of the line
entrusted to them; the policy of the French,
though not then well understood, appeared to

be to withdraw when attacked and counter-
attack. The Americans further had not yet
had time to become accustomed either to their
ground or to their weapons, the Machine Gun
Company, which had two guns in the western
outskirts of the village, and one near the Moulin des Tocs, having also been very recently re-
armed with Hotchkiss guns in place of the
Vickers, and very insufficiently armed with
automatic pistols—only three to the squad of
eight having been issued. In reference to the
time required for preparing Americans to meet
the German armies in the field it is worth noting that though many of these men had trained
for nine months as soldiers, yet, due to this exchange of arms, they first entered the line with
weapons with which less than fifty per cent of
their teams were familiar. This on the 807th
front was the setting for the brief drama; with
the 808th on the right at Badonviller the results obtained indicated much the same conditions.

About three A. M. of the twenty-fourth, a
single shell came wailing in from over the
Saillant du Feys and exploded near the church;

two more followed, and then the storm burst.
It extended over the Grand Bois des Haies on
the left, through St. Maurice and the Bois de
la Voivre, heavily mixed with gas, back across
the Bois des Champs and over Badonviller on
the right, with a storm-center and a box-barrage over Neuviller. The men ducked to the
nearest shelter and waited; they waited too
long, and they had done better not to have
ducked. The rocket signal for counter-barrage brought a total of forty-two shells only
from allied artillery. After nearly an hour
of intense fire, the shelling ceased on the town,
though still continuing around and behind it;
there was hoarse shouting in the darkness, and
then the Germans attacked. They attacked
with rifles, hand-grenades, light machine-guns
strapped to the back, heavy machine-guns from
low-flying aeroplanes, aeroplane-bombs, and
with flame-throwers; and they came in from
the northwest and up the swamp from the
southeast. A confused fight took place in the
gray of dawn through the dense smoke of the
echoing ruins. The French had for the most
part withdrawn at the first opportunity; the

Americans, broken into scattered groups amidst the maze of trenches, wire hurdles, and barricades, fought the best of their way back to the St. Maurice road; a number were caught in the dugouts and shelters, and bombed or burned to death; the head of the communication trench was held by a German light machine-gun firing down it to prevent reënforcement. A stand was made at the western stone barricade to cover the scattered retreat, and the black tar-like stains over its front, with a few charred rifle-barrels from which the stocks had been burned away, bore evidence to the nature of the attack upon it. The report of a machine-gun lieutenant to the captain of that company gives a few interesting details:

"The guns were in emplacements in the extreme west end of the village, flanking its north front, and about one hundred yards apart, the rear gun with no infantry support and the forward gun with two chauchat rifles nearby. At 2:45 A. M. all were asleep in a dugout near the rear gun except one American and one French sentinel at each gun.

"While returning to C. R. Neuviller (i. e.,

Buisson) by trench, and when in rear of Moulin des Tocs I was sniped at twice, one shot hitting the top of the parapet in front of me. I had just arrived at the C. R. when at 8:05 A. M. the barrage started. I aroused my platoon sergeant and we went to M. G. A-20 (enfilading the east front of the village). This gun was in action despite the fact that several gas-shells were landing close to its emplacement. We then tried to get over to Neuviller, but were stopped by a Boche auto-rifle, which was firing from the village along the trench. It was strapped to the back of one Boche who lay prone while it was fired by another. Their contact planes were especially active right above us, and I counted six at one time. We were forced then to lie in the trench and wait. At about 5:45 A. M. three sharp blasts of a whistle were heard from the village, which must have been their signal for withdrawal. The barrage had ceased and we now entered the village. Here I found considerable confusion and a number of wounded, to whom we gave what assistance was possible, and arranged for men to assist them to the C. R. I then visited the gun positions. At the rear gun I found two men still on duty, although the emplacement was so badly knocked to pieces by shells

51

that it was useless. At the forward gun I found five Americans and three Frenchmen. Two Americans and two French were missing —the former, I learned, when the barrage opened, had remained in the dugout, which was gradually filling up with soldiers seeking refuge there. When the barrage lifted these two came out of the dugout and met Boches armed with hand grenades. They fought their way through them, one with his pistol, and the other, being unarmed, with his fists. An auto-rifle opened on them from a position near the barricade about 75 yards up the street and he who was unarmed got out of the village by the rear road; the other lay down in the gutter and opened fire with his pistol. He had emptied one magazine when a Boche with an auto-rifle came out of the alley-way to his right, and, swinging around on his stomach, he emptied the next magazine at him, and he believes he got him. Having no more ammunition he then left the village. Meanwhile the Boches had thrown two grenades into the doorway of the dugout and then began with liquid fire. A corporal slammed the door, and they held it shut till the liquid fire had burned through it, when three men rushed out past the Boches and into the street to the forward gun position, which succeeded in firing about a hundred rounds while the Boches were withdrawing."

"A" Company, in support, had sent up a runner who succeeded in penetrating the barrage and, though wounded, returned with some account of what was going on in the village. At daylight the company, with some French troops, counter-attacked, but found the battle ground deserted, the Germans having, however, taken time to rifle and destroy the stores of the "D" Company kitchen and to remove their own casualties. One German, a sergeant, shot dead in the central square, and another, transfixed by a French bayonet in the outer wire, were all that remained. "D" Company reckoned seven killed, twenty-five wounded, and three missing; "C" Company, one killed, and two wounded from artillery fire; while "B" Company, working through the ensuing day about the shell holes of St. Maurice, had seventy men gassed. The left company of the 808th had, except for those gassed, still heavier losses. Of the number of enemy engaged in the *coup-de-main* no fair estimate can be formed, though information from American prisoners, taken at this time and returned after the armistice, fairly indicates that a special force was brought from elsewhere for the attack, departing by train from Cirey the next day, and that their losses, incurred for the most part by machine-gun fire during their withdrawal, were quite unexpectedly heavy. One man of "D" Company, whose discretion had never been questioned, spent the entire period of enemy occupation beneath the company rolling kitchen, maintaining a strategic silence while the kitchen stores were being looted, and even while the kitchen itself was being blown up with grenades. He emerged to greet the counter-attacking troops of "A" Company, and seemed to claim a certain distinction at not having been driven from his post by the whole of the Hindenberg Circus, which he had faced (?) single-handed.

On the night of July twenty-eighth, the Second Battalion took over the line, the Third Battalion moving to Vacqueville, Xermamont and Les Carrières, and the First Battalion to

BACCARAT—THE WAKE OF EARLY INVASION

Haxo Barracks at Baccarat. On July eighth the Third Battalion took the front. During this time there had been little or no activity beyond nightly patrols into the vast desert of No Man's Land, where enemy patrols were seldom encountered, and never at close range, and where the principal danger faced was from the somewhat nervous fire of both French and American outposts. Patrols occasionally penetrated the enemy lines, in search of prisoners, at the Saillant du Feys and the Arc de Montreux, but without encountering resistance. They were usually ordered so to penetrate and reported having done so—in good faith but often with doubtful accuracy, for in that labyrinth of old wire, crumbling trenches, unmapped trails and willow thickets it was difficult in the darkness to be sure of position. By this time the garrison at Neuviller had been reduced by half, with orders to fall back on Buisson as soon as seriously attacked; the remainder of the right forward company carried the outpost line from the Moulin des Tocs southeast along the edge of the Bois de la Voivre, and formed a first line of support, as

55

yet unmarked by works, across the swamp
meadows of the Blette to the Faiencerie. The
Line 1 bis of support, actually of resistance,
ran along the north and eastern edge of the
Bois des Champs to its extremity at the railroad, with Company Headquarters at Le
Creux Chene, forming a switch line with that
of the forward company. The left forward
company stretched across the Bois des Haies
toward Anceviller, with a joint-post near the
Maré and its support company north of St.
Maurice.

On July fifteenth came word that the long-
expected German blow had fallen on the
Marne, bringing something of relief to the
troops of Lorraine, and on the sixteenth the
French were withdrawn from the sector. An
incident of this withdrawal, as given in a letter at the time, is worth recording:

"The withdrawal of the French, involving a
considerable extension of our front to right
and left with a reassignment of limits, had been
ordered for 9 P. M. that evening, but up till
noon we had received no orders as to that reassignment. When the orders had come, and

I had studied them for a while, the French captain, of whom I had grown quite fond, a curious-looking individual with brilliantly bald head, very long nose, and, in spite of their regulations, crimson breeches, came over to ask if everything was clear. I admitted some difficulties since the orders had overestimated the strength of my company, but told him that we would make out. He considered for a while with his finger beside his nose and then made this extraordinary speech: 'The orders to me,' he said, 'are to have withdrawn my whole command by nine this evening, but I have not yet issued any to my men, as I wanted first to be sure that you would be all right. Unless you assure me that you are, I will give no orders to-night. I am not of the regular service; I have done enough to establish my reputation; and I don't much care what my colonel thinks of me; but I will be d——d if I will go off and leave you in a hole. With another French officer I would probably not feel so, and would tell him that his difficulties were not of my making and he must do his best with them; but I can't do that to an American. So say the word and I stay.'

"I am sure that the proper procedure would have been to kiss him on either cheek, but I couldn't risk the technique. Of course I did not say the word, and that evening, after I had taught him an English drinking song, which he greatly admired but seemed incapable of mastering, he marched away through the woods, still humming it wrong. I missed him greatly and the pleasant meals we had had together in the little rustic summer-house with the rose bushes, at the edge of the vast oak wood and the open meadows of the Blette; and I missed, too, the long midnight talks in our sheet-iron hut in the greenwood, when he had taught me all that his long experience could tell of the war.

"That night I withdrew the whole garrison of Neuviller, save one outpost in the west end of town, establishing a new platoon headquarters at St. Agathe. We crept out in silent procession over the starlit meadows, picking our way across the wake of the old box-barrage, which showed like a line of trenches in the darkness. It was important that the enemy should not know that the village would be left empty at night. I walked at the head of the column with a sergeant clasping to his breast the huge strombos horn used for alarms of a wave-gas attack, and, having jumped the brook, asked him if he could make it. 'Easily, sir,' he answered, as he fell flat on his chest across it, and 'Boo-oo-om' went the great horn, echoing out across the silent meadows, while, over the wide battalion, startled soldiers snatched on their gas-masks and prepared for death. When at last we had choked it off we could only sit where we were and laugh till we were tired."

In the succeeding days there seemed a marked increase of enemy activity. Reports were constant of Germans seen at dark along the Blette; winking flash-lights were sometimes seen at night in the Bois des Champs behind the lines; and both by day and night there came spasmodic auto-rifle fire from No Man's Land upon the outpost line. Yet conclusions were never reached by the nightly patrols, and though one patrol under the captain of "A" Company penetrated as far to the east as the Tranchee Philemon, the only prisoners captured were three who surrendered themselves at the church in Neuviller after living there, between unsuccessful efforts at surrender, for nearly a day and a night. An earlier German patrol in the village, meeting one from men unfamiliar with the outpost positions, had by tact and a judicious use of English obtained the password for the night and gratefully withdrawn; but to this day the subject cannot be safely mentioned to the Battalion Scout Officer whose patrol it was.

It having been determined that on July twenty-first the Americans should launch a blow, at 2 P. M. of that day, the First Battalion again holding the line, Captain Barrett of "B" Company led out some fifty men through the thick woods on the left front to the Barricade du Carrefour. A way had been cut through the very heavy wire in front, but there was no artillery preparation, and the raid was conducted in broad daylight—presupposing a thinly held enemy line and surprise. Whether or not the enemy had obtained advance information, or merely had accomplished very quickly their preparations after warning from scouts, it is impossible to determine. The American force had advanced several hundred yards, and, after cutting through the heavy wire before the Barricade du Carrefour, had passed along it to the right, when, in the silence, came the clear notes of a German bugle. Like the clarion blare of trumpets, when the curtain rose on an old-world pageant, that brief tragedy opened. A line of German infantry rose up in a trench in front; enfilading machine-guns opened up on either flank, and across the wire auto-rifles fired from the trees in rear. To the undying credit of Captain Barrett be it said that he ordered and led a charge. His one lieutenant, with a third of the men, was sent to cut through the wire to the rear, while the remainder of the force, against hopeless odds, tried to clear the front. Poor, brave, beloved Captain Barrett, with his little silk Confederate flag folded in his breast pocket, to fly from the first enemy trench captured— never was the flag of the Lost Cause more gallantly borne, nor to more utter disaster. Of that charging line not one man came back, the captain reeling from a wound and staggering on to death, and of those taken prisoner only one was unwounded. But the others, the lieutenant and sixteen men, came through, and two were unhurt. The score of the First Battalion was mounting.

Captain Barrett, it was said by prisoners, was buried with full military honors at Montreux, toward which place another raid was now being prepared by the regiment. A provisional company was formed from the Third Battalion, then at Haxo Barracks, a picked platoon being sent with one lieutenant from each company for rehearsal at Vacqueville. Save for their inexperience this was probably as fine a body of troops as was ever turned over to a captain for any enterprise—and they were keen, fearfully keen. The ground selected by brigade for the attack lay adjacent to that "B" had traversed, where the wire was very heavy and in places over five feet high. Perhaps this was the reason that the order for attack was cancelled, but in any case after three days at Vacqueville the men were returned to their companies.

The First Battalion had done a second and prolonged turn of duty on the line; the Headquarters Company, with its Stokes mortars and one-pound cannon, and the Machine Gun Company, had never left the line at all, when, on the night of the twenty-ninth, began the relief of the regiment by the 146th Infantry, 37th Division, the latter taking over first the support positions. The Second Battalion took over the front from the First Battalion on the thirtieth and were themselves relieved by the 146th on the night of August third. "B" Company had been temporarily relieved by "E" for three days after its costly attack, and had recruited from the rest of the regiment. The battalions marched out, the Third on the night of August second, 23 kilometers to Giriviller, the Second on the night of the third to Badmenil, and the First on the night of the fourth to Serainville. They were exhausting nights of endless hills, and on one, almost at its most exhausting stage, when sore feet had become an agony and the burden of heavy packs intolerable, when hope no longer suggested that each hill might be the last, nor that there was any last hill to hope for, when sullen or cursing men began to throw themselves down by the roadside—there came out of the darkness a voice. It was a cheerful voice, albeit somewhat drunken, and its drunken cheerfulness was as persistent as only such can be. Its

owner had in court-martial for persistent
drunkenness already forfeited his entire pay
for many months both past and future, and
yet he remained cheerful.

"You can't beat Company ——," he an-
nounced to the darkness. "We've got the officers and we've got the men. So what more
d'you want? What you all groanin' about?
Don't like soldiering? Well, you're gettin'
paid fer it, ain't yer?" Then, with immense
pride: "But I'm not gettin' paid fer it. I'm
doin' this fer nothin', I am—just fer nothin'.
Ev'ry month when I come to the pay-table
Captain calls me a 'optimist,' and that's all
I get paid. Yes, sir, doin' all this fer nothin',
but you don't hear me complainin', do yer?
We've got the officers and we've got—all right,
sir, I won't say another word; only you can't
beat Company ——, can you, sir? We've got
the officers and we've got the men, so what
more do you want?" The Government was
confiscating all his pay, but he was worth three
men's pay to the Government.

From these stations the battalions moved
again to Remenoville and Clezentaine, and in

BACCARAT—A POMPEIAN EFFECT OF STATUES AMID THE RUINS

these areas remained till August seventh. Then came a pleasant daylight march through the sunny forest of Charmes to a bivouac among the beeches of its southwestern edge; and on the eighth the regiment entrained at Charmes for the Marne. The night of the ninth was spent in and about La Ferté Gaucher, at St. Simeon, and Jouy-sur-Marne, and at noon of the tenth the troops were loaded on motor busses for the north. It was an interesting though exhausting twelve-hour ride through the wake of recent battles—the half-ruined villages, the huddled rifle-pits, the shell craters, graves, and the trampled wheat-fields where the charging feet had passed. Château-Thierry was already filling with civilians, patient old men and women returning to their gutted and windowless homes, amidst the still persistent odor of decay.

CHAPTER IV

THE CHÂTEAU DU DIABLE

THE regiment arrived toward midnight at
Fère-en-Tardenois, groping its way on foot
through the block of traffic in the ruined town
to the wooded hill above, and sleeping broadcast through the bushes where the German
dead had not yet all been gathered. At dawn
of the twelfth, the Third Battalion marched
out to take position on the as yet undefined
Blue Line, or second line of resistance, along
the front of the Bois de Voizelle. The great
French and American counter-attack, launched
on July eighteenth along the Marne, had
slowed down to a check along the Vesle, and,
though a bloody way was yet to fight toward
the Aisne, something approaching definite and
organized lines were being established. "I"
Company on the right took position along the
northeast and eastern edge of the woods, overlooking Les Cruaux; "M" on the left stretched

along the northern edge and over the open through Dole to Les Batis Ferme, beyond which was the 158rd Brigade. Battalion Headquarters with "K" and "L" lay in the Bois de la Pisotte.

"M" Company arrived first on its chosen ground as tired and hungry as usual, and with an equally customary lack of prospect of any cooked meal for the remainder of the day. But there was found a battery of artillery from another division with headquarters in these woods, whose officer, with the utmost hospitality, provided a hot meal for the entire company; and an organization that could, without the slightest warning, necessity, or apparent difficulty, off-handedly feed two hundred extra and hungry men suggested a condition of ration supply incredible to the minds of the 807th Infantry.

Save for an unwelcome fieldful of noncombatant, but increasingly unneutral, horses, and the fickle policy of their adherent millions of flies, this situation was, for the two forward companies, at least, very delightful. The Bois de la Pisotte had been too extensively lived in and died in by both Germans and horses, and was rather completely spoiled; but the Bois de Voizelle confined its relics for the most part to cooking utensils, feather quilts, and steel helmets, with the latter of which it was almost paved, that being apparently the article which the German always first discards when hurried. The organization of the ground for defence formed a most interesting task, untrammeled by suggestions or interference from above, and undertaken in the spirit of creative art—somewhat leisurely, first because it was known that the ground would never have to be defended, and second because, when the engineers found time to give it their attention, they were certain to alter all dispositions. This they eventually did, and, to the staunch opinion of all company officers, greatly for the worse; but, in the meantime, enfilading positions were dug in echelon, covered approaches arranged, interlocking belts of fire sighted, and interesting chauchat positions constructed in the trees to cover bits of dead ground. The company commander on the left, having convinced himself that the post of danger lay in the deserted hamlet of Dole, selected its prettiest and most rose-covered cottage for his home, furnishing it from the wide antiquity shop provided in the surrounding orchards.

The weather was immaculate, and had been so almost continuously for three months past; and at evening one would sit at the edge of the woods, looking out over the broad valley, picking out with glasses the new artillery positions established on the farther heights, and watching the similar efforts of the German shells, searching over the grassy slopes or bursting with clouds of white smoke or pink tile-dust in the hillside village of Chery Chartreuve or the farms. Occasionally a weird form of projectile would burst with a mass of black smoke high in the air, to be followed the next instant by a leaping fountain of flames from the ground beneath, and sometimes one that gave vent to two, three, or even four separate explosions on the ground. Toward sundown the hostile aeroplanes would come over, in twos or threes, for an attack on the observation balloons, very often successful, and would turn back from their flaming victim scarcely bothering to rise out of range above the drumming machine-guns; nor did they ever seem to pay the penalty for their bravado. At nightfall dim columns of artillery and transport would wind down the hill, with the gleam of helmets moving ghostlike through a fog of moonlit dust; the whirr of enemy motors would grow in the darkness overhead, the swish and shock of falling bombs with extravagant pineapple forms of fire springing from the earth; or from the misty valley-bottom, where the heavy artillery was thundering, would come the red flare of explosions, hoarse shoutings and the blowing of claxton gas-alarms. It was a wonderful pageant of war, spread daily before one's eyes, to be watched with all the apparent safety of the theater-goer.

Once, at noon, two American planes were seen circling directly overhead, and, a thousand feet above them, three Germans against the blue. A faint splutter of shots was heard, but the distance was far too great for effective fire, and the danger of the Americans did not seem imminent when they were seen suddenly to crash together and the wing of one to shear off at the shoulder. Down it dropped, dropped, dropped, slowly, swiftly, and then with appalling speed, gathering impetus with every fathom, nose first, in one plummeting chute, the sunshine gleaming on its painted sides and the whirr of its motor growing to a deafening roar, sliding like a lost soul through thousands of feet of air, a glistening, living thing headed for utter destruction; and it struck, in a pile of crumpled débris, at the edge of the wood. The other, reeling from the blow, came down in a staggering spiral, almost under control, fouled in the top of some cottonwoods below the hill, and turned end-over on to the ground. Each had carried only a single man, and Lieutenants Smythe and Wallace were buried side by side in the Bois de Voizelle.

The pleasant time of sunshine and ease and almost disinterested observation was soon over, the pleasanter in retrospect for it never occurred again. The Division had relieved both the 4th American and the 62nd French Divisions on the line, the 305th Infantry taking over at first the entire divisional front. Four days later the 308th had taken over from it

MAP
of
·VESLE-AISNE·
·AUG·12 – SEPT·16·
·1918·
Scale of kilometres

the right half, as forming the sector of the
154th Brigade; the 28th Division lay on the
right in Fismes. The Red Line, or Line of
Resistance, in this brigade sector followed approximately the crest of a high ridge along the
southern edge of the Bois de Cochelet—a dense
wood of small birch-trees springing from a
subsoil of chalk. Beyond the northern foot of
the ridge, where the woods again ceased, the
land stretched in an open grassy plateau, dot-
ted here and there with small orchards, to the
steep and wooded declevities of the valley
proper. This was perhaps half-a-mile's width
of swampy bottom-land—meadow, marsh, and
willow-scrub—across which the Vesle, a river
some thirty feet broad and six or eight feet
deep, looped back and forth. Beyond the valley to the north the open hills rose higher toward the Aisne, and beyond it again culminat-
ed in the great commanding ridge of the Che-
min des Dames, for which the French and
Germans had wrestled for years. Everything
forward, and a good deal that was back of the
Red Line lay completely open to enemy observation and fire; the position for the support-

ing troops formed a practically insoluble problem; there could be no reënforcement nor supply of the front except at night, nor was there
any natural cover from the very searching artillery fire. This, several times a day, would
comb out the length of the valley's rim, where
was the only woodland; and any movement in
daylight of even one or two men across the
open table-land would draw a sniping fire of
77's.

On the night of August eighteenth, the
Third Battalion moved forward, relieving the
Third Battalion of the 808th on the Red Line
in the Bois de Cochelet, and itself relieved by
the Second Battalion from Dravegny. The
First Battalion, which had remained in the
Boise de Saponay, above Fère-en-Tardenois,
till the fourteenth, was already in the Bois de
la Pisotte. Save once, and then seemingly by
chance, in the woods beside Baccarat, no part
of the Third Battalion had as yet been under
shell-fire; and "K" and "L" Companies, along
the eastern edge of the Bois de Cochelet, were
still comparatively immune; but "M" and "I,"
bordering its south on the high ground, soon

came in for their share. Batteries of six-inch howitzers were in position beneath the fringe of pine trees under the crest of the hill; and huddled under their very muzzles the companies dug into the hard chalk. One platoon of "M" was at first placed in the little wood between Les Prés and Resson Farms, to maintain liaison with the 28th Division on the right —a liaison that was never maintained for more than twenty-four consecutive hours before it was found that the latter had disappeared, and scouting parties would be sent to search for them. The front edge of the wood being lined with 75's, it was constantly searched by enemy fire, and the platoon was moved to Resson Farm, whose medieval vaults, when not filled with water, offered the only effective shelter of the Red Line.

The woods along the hill crest were indescribably filthy with the refuse of former occupation, and haunted by incalculable flies. The narrow rifle-pits and half-finished trenches of the men, covered with branches and shelter-halves loaded with chalk, as protection against shell fragments, being compara-

tively clean and cool, did not seem an especially attractive resort for the fair-minded fly,
particularly in view of the lavish banquet
spread broadcast through the woods; but the
flies felt differently about it and were very
determined. A man would crawl into his shelter, with a leafy branch in either hand, and,
lying on his back, would begin threshing above
his face, gradually working down the length
of his body. As the aperture was approached
the flies would become desperate, charging
back at the waving branches, and facing death
by scores rather than suffer ejection. When
this process had been two or three times repeated a sufficient clearance would be effected
to enable the man perhaps to get to sleep before the place again filled up. At night they
hung in black masses over the walls and roof,
noisily propagating their species through the
hours of darkness, and every crashing discharge of the 155's overhead would bring down
an avalanche of chalk and flies. The yellow
wasps were only really bothersome when an
issue of jam arrived, at which times it was

practically impossible to separate the two long enough to eat one without the other.

Just why the infantry were held, inactive but permanent, directly under the muzzles of the guns, drawing observation upon the artillery while the latter drew fire upon the infantry, was never made evident to either party of the unwilling combination. The shelling of this area was systematic but far from severe, and seemed intended mostly for the batteries. Had it been otherwise, congested as the men were in their improvised shelters, the losses might have been appalling. It consisted for the greater part of three-inch H. E. (high explosive), much of it with overhead bursts, and of sneezing gas. Every precaution was taken to keep the men under cover during daylight, but the ration details, carrying the two meals a day from the company kitchens at Chery-Chartreuve, were a constant source of danger. The platoon at Resson Farm, alone, however, was under observation by balloons. A line of trenches had been laid out on the lower ground of the Bois de Mont St. Martin, where the thick trees seemed to offer adequate protection from observation, and work upon them was begun by details from the four companies. Three German planes were seen through the leaves hovering high overhead and soon the shells began ranging in. So accurate was the fire and efficient the observation that, among the first half-dozen shells, one broke on the lip of the trench, wounding four men, who lay prone along its bottom. Chery-Chartreuve, a mile to the southwest, where the company kitchens were located, concealing their smoke in empty barns, came in for its daily bombardment. A fair description of the place may be quoted from a letter written at the time:

"There had been shelling as usual in Chery that morning, and the outhouse next to our company kitchen, where some of the ration-detail were sleeping, had been blown to pieces. A runner came up to get replacements for the detail, and reported that two of the men had been hurt and a third had disappeared; the roof had fallen in, and, though he seemed to feel sure that the missing man was not under it, he did not speak very convincingly about it, so I went down to see what I could find. It was a day of breathless heat, and the white road was padded with dust. I passed a steep hillslope of empty funk-holes, looking like a great rabbit-warren, or a village of cliff-dwellers, and in spite of the two robust-looking horses at its bottom, each with two legs pointing straight to the sky, it struck me as a very preferable location for our men. The roadside was littered with chauchat-magazines, carriers, and cartridge-belts, half hidden in the dust. The village lay lifeless beneath the sun, a thin white fog of dust from some recent shelling hanging above it, and the taint of gas in the air. In the ruined outhouse was a sidecar, rather badly damaged, beneath which the missing man, an Italian, was supposed to have been sleeping—though I couldn't see why he had selected it. It was a relief that the débris of the tile roof did not look enough to conceal a man. To make sure, however, we lifted off such beams as there were, but without raising anything beyond a cloud of tile-dust mixed with mustard-gas.

"There didn't seem to be anywhere else to look for him, since the surgeon who had dressed the other two knew nothing of him, and I concluded that eventually he would be, as eventually he was, reported from hospital through

some unexpected channel; but now as I stood
looking up the blistering way to our hilltop
that I had to travel, my eye was caught at the
turn of the road by a long, roofed, stone-
flagged washing-place, such as the French
blanchisseuses use all over the land. In a moment I was beside it, and in another moment
I was in it. It was full to the brim with clear
cold water, four feet deep in the middle and
twenty feet long, and the sheer joy of that
swim I shall never forget. I hadn't seen so
much water together in one place since I left
the ocean. After that the mess-sergeant
cooked me a meal with a lot of delicious fresh
vegetables he had gotten from somewhere, and
I went back up what we called Shrapnel Hill
with the feeling of having spent a week-end at
the seashore."

Les Prés Farm, where the first-aid station
was established close under the hill, was sub-
jected to a constant and accurate fire, so that
it became increasingly a matter of wonder that
the place held together. Almost every day a
few were wounded, the sight of the stretcher-
bearers carrying their burdens down the slope
becoming too familiar to cause any comment

beyond a question as to the man's company. Dysentery too became everywhere prevalent. Water was scarce, and the days were long and irksome with the glare of heat from the sun-scorched chalk. But at night a glamor spread over the mist-filled valley, with its stabbing white flashes of artillery and red flare of ex-plosions. Once an ammunition dump of 75's was fired in the open, and continued all through the night, sending its empty shell-cases wail-ing about like banshees through the darkness. Once, on a still night of midsummer moon-shine there passed a strange flight of projec-tiles, like a flock of migrating birds, high, high up in the moonlit silence, coming from one knew not where, and traveling with a drowsy note and on even keel to some remote target far in the inaudible distance.

On the night of August twenty-fifth, the Second Battalion, leap-frogging the Third, took over the front line from the 308th. The next day a battalion attack was ordered for dawn of the twenty-seventh. The front of the regimental sector at this time ran along the south bank of the Vesle through the woods due

north of Villesavoye, crossed the river on a
footbridge and followed north along the west
edge of the woods to the railroad, passed under
the tracks through an open culvert, the track
itself being swept by enemy enfilade fire of
machine-guns, and occupied the southwest corner of the woods beyond. A switch line ran
east along the track, and, though not continuously, south along the eastern edge of the wood
to the Vesle once more. Another and isolated
position was held a kilometer to the east at the
Tannerie. Battalion Headquarters as originally taken over from the 308th was in a dugout on the steep wooded slope southwest of
Villesavoye, but, on account of the continuous
shelling of this area, was changed to a large
cave on the high ground south of the Tannerie.
The dressing station was in another cave on a
bluff south of Villesavoye, readily distinguished in the distance by the continuous bursting of shells at its mouth. Very little inter-
communication was possible between the various portions of the line, and this only by
devious routes. Both flanks were very open
and ill-defined, and much of the ground was

82

debatable. Maps of the region were scarce, were all of very small scale, and of a particularly perishable quality of paper. There were some, but not all, made with two systems of superimposed non-parallel coördinate lines— all leading to very possible errors in the locating of positions. An incident in this connection is worth mentioning when an officer of the Third Battalion, on August twenty-fourth, previous to the receipt of the order for the leap-frogging of that battalion by the Second, going fórward to reconnoitre the position of the right forward company, was provided with a guide supposed, more than any other, to be familiar with that ground. The guide conducted the officer in broad daylight into No Man's Land and onto the muzzles of a German machine-gun nest beneath the concrete signal-house, having previously been restrained, only by the growing pessimism of the officer, from scaling the railroad embankment at a point where its opposite side was afterwards found to be lined with enemy rifle-pits. In justice be it said, however—for the man was as brave a soldier as he was inefficient a guide

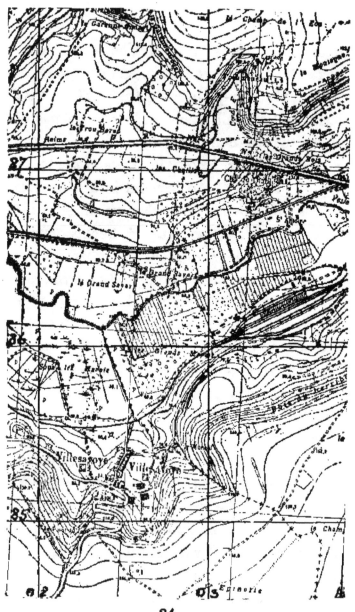

84

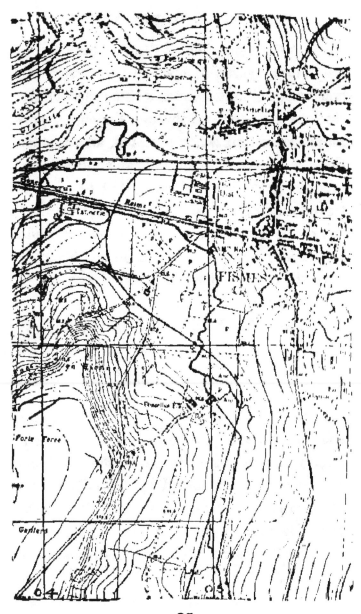

—that when lying behind a single bush across only eighty yards of open meadow from the machine-gun position, with a bullet through the stock of his rifle, two through the empty ammunition box on which it rested, and another through his shoulder, his only thought was for redeeming the trust which he felt he had betrayed; and he continually urged that he crawl out to the north to draw the enemy fire while the officer make his escape to the south. Fortunately a more cheerful solution was eventually reached.

The order for this attack of the Second Battalion gave as its purpose the "retaking of all positions lost by the 308th Infantry," and defined as its objective the crossing of the railroad with the Rouen-Reims national highway and the Château du Diable—ground which, while in enemy hands menacing the river valley, was itself dominated by the hills to the north, and was well-nigh as difficult to hold as it was to take while the hills were held in force by the enemy. The two platoons at the Tannerie, in the few yards of ground between the road and the river, had a lookout stationed immediately north of the national highway, but the latter itself was swept and commanded by enemy fire from either flank. The Château du Diable rose on a precipitous slope of woods filled with accordion-wire, dominating the low-lying swamps and willow-thickets to the south. For the rest, the whole region had been fought and fought over by the 4th, the 82nd, and the 28th Divisions. Every wood and march was filled with cast-off equipment and the broken wreckage of war; St. Thibault, Villesavoye, Bazoches, and Fismes, all were unspeakable with the human débris of unsuccessful or inconclusive attacks—flotsam and jetsam cast upon the dreary shores where the tides of victory had ebbed and flowed.

The absence of any clear knowledge as to the enemy's strength or dispositions—for little of this could here be gathered from the troops relieved—the very vague and non-continuous character of the line, and the lack of any natural position of strength or shelter, from which assault might be launched, or to which, in case of unsuccess, withdrawal might be made, rendered the coming attack, delivered as it was to be within the first twenty-four hours of occupation of the line, undoubtedly hazardous. Major Jay, it should be said, threw the whole weight of his influence toward obtaining at least a postponement—but other counsels prevailed.

A paragraph of the official report made after the attack may be quoted at length:

"At a conference held at the forward battalion P. C. (Poste de Commande) during the afternoon, Major Jay, commanding the Second Battalion, stated that he did not feel it was possible for him to reconnoitre and prepare properly to make the attack on the morning of the twenty-seventh, as had been suggested, and requested that the hour be delayed until the morning of the twenty-eighth. An additional reason for this request was the fact that the supporting artillery of this Regiment was assisting an operation of the 153rd Brigade on the night of 26th-27th August and would not be available to support an operation in our sector. It was determined, however, that the attack would be made on the morning of the twenty-seventh, and Lieutenant-Colonel Benjamin, commanding the Regiment, received instructions, copies of which are at-

88

tached hereto, to that effect. He immediately notified Major Jay."

A prisoner captured that day by the 112th Infantry at Fismes brought word that a German general attack along the sector was preparing for the morning of the twenty-seventh —which promised ill for the reception of the Second Battalion. An officer of "F" Company went out to reconnoitre the ground for a possible attack upon the Château from the Tannerie on the east. He was injured by a shell, and a second officer volunteered for the task. But from the east the only way lay over the open marsh where "C" Company of the 308th had been cut to pieces in a similar and fruitless attempt, and it was determined to attack from the west.

At about 2 A. M. of the twenty-seventh the Major held a conference in a little dugout by the railroad culvert, where their duties were assigned to the four company commanders. "H," lying north of the tracks, was to attack the Château, "E" to attack along the tracks to the railroad crossing, "F" to move in support, and

89

"G" to guard the left from counter-attack. Zero hour was set for 4:15 A. M.

It was still dark when they started, and low over Bazoches to westward hung the thread of a dying moon, while beneath it grew the dull roar of the attack of the 158rd Brigade. Shells were passing overhead, but all toward Bazoches. Through dense swamp the leading platoons moved forward in column, and at the edge of the open meadow deployed in line. Less than a hundred yards of wet grass in the gray of morning, and beyond it the thicker darkness of unknown woods. A Very light shot up on the left, calling for such artillery as was to aid. An enemy smoke bomb exploded on the tracks in front, blotting out whatever movement of troops occurred behind, and then the machine guns opened. From the Château to the river the woods seemed alive with them, for it was not for nothing that the enemy had prepared their attack upon that very ground at the same hour, and upon a scale intended to insure success. A regiment was massed upon that slope of woods, and with it two extra machine gun companies—perhaps fifty guns in all

90

—and against them "H" and "E" Companies advanced to the attack. They did not know the odds against them—it was not known until after the war—they only knew that they were struck by such a blast of fire as made life impossible. That part of "H" which attempted the open meadow was swept away, while the rest, gaining only a few rods through the neck of woods, there clung under a steady hail of bullets.

"E" Company, on the right, not facing the main position, at first did better. They crossed the first stretch of meadow to the line of trees and flung one platoon across the tracks, then, astride the tracks, they crossed the second meadow. Their leading platoons disappeared in the woods beyond, and for a while the rest waited. The fire was appalling, crossing from the hill to the river and sweeping down the tracks. After a little the platoon to the south, losing direction in the thick swamp, reappeared, and, to give it time to reform, its support platoon attacked through it. Nothing was heard of that to the north under Lieutenant O'Brien, and of runners sent to that cor-

ner of woods those who returned reported that
there was nothing there but German machine
guns. It was gone, and not a man of it came
back. Captain Adams of "E" and Lieutenant
Scudder, starting in search of it, fell side by
side, each shot through the neck as they lifted
their heads above the railroad embankment.
Major Jay, a hundred yards down the track,
dropped with a broken arm, and, after a brave
effort to retain his command, was carried back.
Captain Davis of "F" then took command, but
no one could judge what was taking place in
that inferno of noise in front. Corporal Hal-
berstadt undertook to find Captain Adams, and
did so, reporting to him when both were prisoners in the German lines. There was fire
from the right and the word spread that it was
chauchat fire—that part of "E's" right platoon which had lost direction was shooting on
them, and, calling that he was going to find out,
Lieutenant Reed, the Battalion Adjutant,
plunged into the woods there. He was not seen
again except by one man, who reported that
he had found him shot through both legs, and
that when he had tried to help him back the

92

lieutenant had told him to bring back the message instead—that it was enemy fire. Then "H" sent word that they could not hold their slender gains without reënforcement, and, almost as the reënforcements from "F" started out, came a second message that "H" had withdrawn.

That finished it, for no further effort was possible for the troops at hand. Another part of "F" had already been sent to clear the woods east along the river, and the danger of a counter-stroke from the west was too great to allow the withdrawal of "G" from their position. South of the tracks the line had been advanced to the strip of trees across the first meadow, but on the north the former positions were resumed. Long afterward a few of the dead were found among the fallen poplars at the base of the Château hill, and some even near the far eastern edge of the woods, but for the most part the battleground was left in the hands of an enemy who glean it well.

The price was heavy—of officers, three wounded and four missing, of whom only one, Captain Adams, returned alive after the arm-

istice, and of men, sixteen killed, eighty-four
wounded and forty missing—one hundred and
forty enlisted men, ten from Battalion headquarters, eleven from "F," twenty-one from
"G," thirty-five from "E," and sixty-three
from "H." Throughout the action, lasting
some two hours, the heavy artillery had played
upon the support positions south of the river
—causing "G" its losses, but overshooting the
rest of the Battalion.

It seems probable that the enemy, taking the
attack in conjunction with that, more costly
and scarcely more successful, of the 153rd
Brigade upon Bazoches, had believed it to be
much stronger than in fact it was, and their
artillery sought only to break up the reserves,
of which, fortunately or unfortunately, there
were none present. Perhaps for the same reason no counter-attack was launched.

The attack of the Second Battalion had
failed, in that neither of its two objectives were
for a moment seriously threatened; and yet,
with the clearer knowledge we now have of that
against which the attack was launched, it may
be that its bloody failure should be reckoned

CONCRETE SIGNAL-HOUSE ON THE RAILROAD TRANSFORMED INTO A GER-
MAN PILL-BOX, SEEN FROM ITS REAR. THE MACHINE-GUN IN ITS
BASEMENT CUT A SWATHE THROUGH THE ATTACK OF THE 2ND BAT-
TALION

THE CHÂTEAU DU DIABLE, LOOKING ACROSS A SIDE BRANCH OF THE VESLE

success—a distant and unconscious parallel to the "Revenge." For the devotion of two companies to their appointed task held immobile before them a force perhaps six or eight times their number that was intended to attack; and the blow they struck against it, however impotent to achieve their purpose, served at least to prevent what might have been a disaster to the battalion and to the line. There can be no estimate of the enemy loss, though to have so completely paralyzed their initiative, it must have been heavy.

A feature of the enemy organization, learned through prisoners of either side, may here be mentioned as of interest; namely, that each German infantry company carried with it normally a section of heavy machine guns, composed originally of eight guns, but at this time reduced to four—whereas the American infantry company, unless by special detail, had none; and that the German company carried also a section, or even platoon, solely for the evacuation of the dead and wounded of both sides during an action. These men were seen going about unarmed upon their task while the attack was at its height, and their activity will largely account for the constant feeling in the American lines that little or no losses were being inflicted upon the enemy. Night of August twenty-seventh saw the regimental sector practically unchanged, while on their left the 158rd Brigade had taken and at terrific cost relost Bazoches, and on their right the 28th Division had been driven from their scanty footing in Fismette.

CHAPTER V

On the night of August twenty-eighth the Third Battalion relieved the Second Battalion on the front line, the latter drawing back to the Bois de la Pisotte and the next night to Sergy. The Third Battalion had by now spent ten days on the Red Line—the days spent largely in trench digging and many of the nights in carrying ammunition from Villesavoye to the forward battalions of the brigade. It was not a period of much physical exhaustion, but the strength of the men was sapped with dysentery, and the shell-fire on the two rear companies had been very constant. In "M" Company, at least, every officer but one was already a casualty, and that remaining lieutenant was killed by a direct hit of a shell on their first day in the forward position. Happily two of the others were able at the same time to return to duty, but at this unfortunate juncture the companies were required to send selected officers and N. C. O.'s away to school.

The tenure of the line by the Third Battalion was not marked by any especial activity, though the losses from artillery and machine-gun fire were very constant, and the life—lying all day in the shallow rifle-pits, eating sparingly of such food as they had brought with them, and drinking the water of the polluted river—was wearing in the extreme. "M" held in the woods beyond the railroad, "L" on the right between the railroad and the river, "K" south of the river, and "I" at the Tannerie, in the narrow strip between river and highway, and, as battalion reserve, on the high ground to the south. Battalion Headquarters' cave was a vast affair of flickering candles and dim recesses, paved with equipment and sleeping soldiers, over which one entering picked his tortuous way. A general attack similar to that made by the Second Battalion was ordered for the Third, but was countermanded at the time Lieutenant-Colonel Houghton assumed command of the regiment.

One short and uncontested advance was, however, made on the left, when, before dawn of the thirty-first, two platoons of "I" Company crept forward across the river and through the swamp and willow-scrub to the railroad-cut north of the Grand Savar. This advance, which was the cause of some newspaper comment at the time, while not complicated, was well handled; the men dug in very quickly on their new line, and no resistance was encountered. The only resultant losses were from causes quite unexpected. The lieutenant in charge had been directed, as soon as his objective had been reached, to send up a six-star rocket in order to bring up the machine guns on his left,—a signal which, at about 4 A. M., brought a very prompt response from the enemy artillery, though widely overshooting their position. But the return fire from the supporting artillery fell as much short, deluging the woods where "M" Company held across the railroad, and causing them four casualties. About 5 P. M. two enemy planes circled very low above the new position occupied by "I" Company; but the men lay close, and there seemed no immediate sequel except, after the departure of the planes, a brief bombardment by friendly artillery with overhead H. E. That night the Third Battalion was relieved by the First, some marching out to the Bois de la Pisotte and thence, after a brief rest, to Sergy, seven kilometers to the south, others being carried there by trucks from Chery-Chartreuve and arriving toward midnight of September first.

The First Battalion had taken over the Blue Line on August twenty-second, and the Red Line on the night of the twenty-fifth, lying to the left of the Third Battalion on either side of the St. Thibaut-Chery-Chartreuve road. This position had been taken up under an interdiction fire from enemy artillery—a statement which inadequately describes the confusion of tired men stumbling about amidst drenching rain, through the thick darkness and underbrush of unfamiliar slopes, and groping under artillery fire for the uncertain protection of rifle-pits. Two were killed and four wounded at this time. On the front line "A" Company took over in the woods north of the rail-

road, "B" immediately south of the tracks, and
"C" along the south bank of the river. A combat group between the Tannerie and Fismes
maintained liaison with the 28th Division on the
right, but in spite of the extension of the line
for two hundred yards to the left along the
railroad, effected by the Third Battalion, no
liaison had been established with the 158rd
Brigade, and the position had there been organized by Captain Hubbell of the Machine-
Gun Company as a defensive flank. Against
this flank an attack was launched early on the
night of September first.

The afternoon and evening had been unusually quiet until, at about 10 P. M., the enemy opened with 77's on the "B" Company positions along the railroad, the fire quickly increasing into a heavy barrage. This lasted
for some twenty minutes, mixed with machine-
gun fire; an American counter-barrage was
laid down in front of the position for about
fifteen minutes; then the enemy attacked from
the northwest with light and heavy machine-
guns, rifle- and hand-grenades. "B" Company
and the machine-gun crews, holding their

ground, fired out into the darkness with every weapon at hand. It seems improbable that targets were at any time visible on either side, and after a quarter of an hour the enemy fire slackened and finally ceased. As in almost all such affairs, no idea could be formed of the enemy loss owing to their very careful gathering of all casualties; none actually reached the American line, which remained intact throughout. "B" Company's loss was only of a single casualty from a rifle-grenade.

At dawn of the second the captain of "A" Company, who had been wandering dazedly about in the woods half the night after being knocked unconscious by a shell, sent out a patrol from the north of his position toward the Château du Diable; but it was met by immediate machine-gun fire from the woods strongly held to the south of the Château, and retired with the loss of one man. A platoon of "A," south of the tracks, was ordered to seize and occupy the point of woods between the north and south bend of the river and the railroad. Filtering in by groups, they succeeded in establishing themselves here for a while, and attempted to surround the first machine-gun position upon which they stumbled; but other guns echeloned to the rear, firing from concealment upon a position well known to them, together with rifle-fire from across the river, drove back the platoon to its original location with a loss of five casualties. This activity on the part of "A" Company seemed to persuade the enemy that a general attack was pending, for an intense artillery fire was laid down on that company's position, killing five and wounding a dozen, beside a few further casualties in "B" and "C."

The French attacks around Soissons were by now bringing pressure on the enemy's right flank, so that he gave indications of a withdrawal on the regimental front. At dawn of September fourth, after a brief artillery preparation, "A" and "C" Companies, under command of Captain Blagden, struck southeast from the north of their position and northeast from the river, meeting along the railroad to the south of the Château. There was no opposition; the woods where "H" and "E" had suffered so fearfully were empty save for their

108

unburied dead, and a scattered few of the enemy outposts whose only thought was of escape. Pushing up the steep slope they found the Château du Diable, with broken windows and hanging doors, also deserted. It was a disappointing place, whose grim name and brooding presence, fortressed by trees, so long dominating the front, would have suggested some gloomy relic of ancient days; but it appeared as a modern and bizarre villa of brick and wood, surrounded by paths of oleander. The companies crossed the Rouen-Reims highroad, under a slight enfilading fire, and, still unopposed, climbed the slopes of the Montagne de Perles to the north, where they dug in below the crest.

The Second Battalion in the meantime, after six days in the rearward area at Sergy and the Blue Line, were now advancing to the right front along the Mont St. Martin-Fismes road, reaching the latter place about dusk, and taking up a temporary position in the ruined cellars of that most desolate town. "E" and "H" Companies, coming in from the left, ran the gauntlet of some artillery fire, but without cas-

SIDE STREET IN FISMES—WATER BACKING UP FROM THE CHOKED RIVER
INTO THE TOWN

THE RIVER FRONT AT FISMES, LOOKING ACROSS THE VESLE FROM FISMETTE

ualties. Captain Blagden here joined them with orders to take command of the battalion and push forward through Fismette to the north.

The troops were massed in the town, whose streets were blocked with tumbled débris and wire, and where every courtyard held its unburied dead. The bridge across the river was reported to have been restored by the Engineers. At 8 P. M. the column started, groping its way forward to the river; the ruins of the bridge were found unrestored, and at the same time enemy artillery opened fire on the road. In complete darkness and under shell-fire a plank bridge was improvised among the remains of the former structure, and the battalion began crossing in single file. One shell struck the bridge directly; another, of large caliber, wiped out almost the entire headquarters personnel, together with two machine-gun officers, Captain Blagden practically alone remaining unhurt. Fourteen were killed and ten wounded by this single explosion, and four of the casualties were officers. Beyond the river the road to Fismette was blocked with piled coils of wire; and still the shells kept searching through the darkness over that desperately slow advance. At last, winning free of the town, the battalion dug in on the side of the sunken road to its north.

At 7 A. M. of September 5th, with a new battalion headquarters organized, the advance was resumed,—"G," which the night before had lost direction and advanced almost to Blanzy-les-Fismes before returning to the Battalion, and "H" on the left, "F" and "E" on the right. As the leading squad-columns reached the high ground by the east and west narrow-gauge line, they were met by machine-gun fire from either flank, and, deploying, attempted to advance by squad rushes. But the fire, increasing in intensity from the near brink of the Ravin Marion, was mixed now with that of heavy machine-guns from the Petite Montagne, a mile and a half to the north, and finally with an artillery barrage upon the skirmish line. The supporting platoons attempted to flank out the nearer positions, but could not advance the line, on which the 28th Division was also found to be held up on the right;

every move brought a new burst of artillery fire, for the whole position was under direct observation from the north, and with already heavy losses the battalion dug in along the embankment of the narrow-gauge line. In this position at noon the battalion was advised that a rolling barrage would be laid down along their front behind which they were directed to advance; but as the afternoon waned, bringing no barrage, a runner was sent back for confirmation of the order. Then at 4:30 came word that the barrage had passed at 10 A. M. and that the advance must begin at once. It was attempted, but at once hurled back by artillery fire.

Liaison was very faulty, and there appears at this time, and for some days thereafter, to have been a radical misconception as to the position of the 28th Division on the right. The Second Battalion was in touch with its left midway between Baslieux and Glennes, yet on the morning of this day a message was written stating that: "The 28th report their left at La Bossette (a kilometer north of Glennes) and desire your assistance in taking La Pe-

tite Montagne. You will coöperate to the full-
est extent. Push forward vigorously with
troops you report near Merval." And again
on the same day: "The 28th Division occu-
pies the northern extremities of spurs on south
bank of the Aisne with patrols in Maizy, Muscourt and Meurival. They report no liaison
with the 154th Brigade. This is probably due
to the more aggressive advance made by that
division. You must at once push your patrols
out to the Aisne and get G. C.'s across same
to the heights on the north."

The conception seemed to the Second Battalion to be over-enthusiastic. The patrols in
Maizy, Muscourt, and Meurival seemed to be
exercising singularly little restraint on the
Germans in and about Glennes; while the
heights north of the Aisne appeared as distant
as, though less sympathetic than, the shores of
America. On the left the leading battalion of
the 308th was dug in north of Blanzy in touch
with "G" Company. Of the accuracy of other
reports there seemed less question, as: "We are
completely out of food and have not had any
since yesterday morning, and very little then.

Please rush the rations. C. O. Company A."

After dark the advance was again begun. "F" and "E" met fierce machine-gun fire from the head of the Ravin Marion, and, leaving a mixed post in an old trench facing its westerly horn, refused this flank. The battalion advanced in column up the road through Merval, its commander acting as point. Across the deep valley to the left Serval was burning furiously, sending up long columns of sparks into the night, and showing the black silhouettes of tree tops that scarcely rose to the brink of the crest on which the battalion moved. To the north was the glow of other fires along the Aisne. Near the road-fork southeast of St. Pierre farm a German sentry was surprised and captured, giving the information that the fork was strongly held by a picket, but that they would likely surrender if given opportunity. It seems probable that the information was given in good faith, and that the capture would have been effected but for the untimely arrival of a German officer who broke off negotiations and drove the patrol of "G"

Company down the road with a burst of machine-gun fire.

Another patrol was sent to the left to regain

the contact lost with the leading elements of the 808th; and after losing half its number in the dense blackness of forest and swamp in the Marais Minard, under a constant explosion of

gas-shells, discovered the forward battalion of
that regiment in a formation something like a
hollow square on the conical Butte de Bour-
mont—a formation appearing a trifle selfish,
and lending itself better to security than to
liaison; but, in such warfare a commander
learned to entrust his flanks to himself. The
battalion huddled itself down for the night
upon the northern end of the spur, and next
day took position with "F," "E" and "H"
stretching from the north, near the eastward
bend of the road, to the sunken road and the
cellars of Merval on the south, "G" outposting
across the Marais Minard toward the 308th,
and battalion headquarters, dressing station,
and the reserve platoons, in two large caves to
the north of the church.

September sixth and seventh passed without notable event beyond a slow but steady
drain of casualties from artillery and machine-
gun fire, and a constant drenching of gas where
"G" lay stretched across the swamp-land. A
fair example of the danger of forwarding reports of patrols is to be found in that of an
efficient N. C. O. who was sent with one man

and careful instructions to attempt an entry into Revillon, and report on dispositions of the enemy. They returned in the course of the night to report that they passed through the town and found it quite empty. This statement, quite sincerely given, was, although remarkable, gaining credence with the battalion commander, when he added the detail that he had met Captain Hubbell of the machine-gun company also wandering about the streets of the place, who had assured him that there was nothing there of interest. In spite of the well-known enterprise of this officer, he was also known to belong on the left, and the thing seemed unlikely, receiving a more satisfactory explanation when Captain Hubbell sent word that he had been in Barbonval. One French name was often a good deal like another to the American enlisted man and direction was hard to keep at night.

There was a constant difficulty of ration supply, both in bringing up the transport at night over the shell-swept road, and in distributing to the outlying platoons. There could be little or no attempt at providing cooked food. A

112

CHURCH AT MERVAL, OVERLOOKING THE ENEMY LINES TO THE NORTH
AND USED AS AMERICAN OBSERVATION POST

BATTALION HEADQUARTERS AT MERVAL, A FORTY-FOOT CAVE IN THE
CHALK

ration-dump had been established near the
Merval church; and then one night it was
changed to the Distillerie, nearly a kilometer
to the south—but without warning of the
change to the forward troops. After a night
of fruitless waiting at the church they got
word of the true state of affairs, and hurried
down to the Distillerie in time to see the entire
ration-dump obliterated by the direct hit of
one six-inch shell. The latter catastrophe was
of course unavoidable; but the lack of coöperation signalized in the first part was far from
rare, and added a burden of hardship which
was more keenly felt than the privations which
were known to be inevitable.

On the evening of September eighth, after
arrangements had been completed for the relief of the Second Battalion by the Third, an
order was received calling for an attack upon
Revillon, La Roche, and Cuchery, reorganiza-
tion upon that ground, and a further advance
to the Bois de Senfontaine and Maizy. The
line of departure from which the advance was
to be made was indicated as approximately
straight from Le Verdillon on the left to cross-

roads 128.2 (at the "G" in "Glennes") on the right; and the rolling barrage behind which it was to move was scheduled for 6:45 P. M. "G" Company was deployed along its line of outposts, "E" across the north end of the Merval ridge, "H" facing east along the sunken road, and "F" behind it in support. "C" and "B" were also brought up to support the left and center. On the left, the line of departure was closely approximated, but on the right was looked upon as a first objective, its indication as a starting-point being a sort of corollary to the myth, still persistent, that the 28th was across the Aisne. At 6:45 all companies started forward. A passing shower blew in from the east, and as the troops deployed upon the open ground they saw the grassy heights of La Petite Montagne through a veil of glistening rain and spanned by a rainbow arch—but there was little of victory in that fair omen, and much of death.

"G" and "C" had no sooner come out upon the meadows beyond Le Verdillon than they were met by a hurricane of shells and machine-gun fire from the sunken road northwest of

St. Pierre farm, from the houses of Revillon, and from the heights of La Petite Montagne. They staggered a short distance forward upon their hopeless way toward the wire lining the road in their front, and then reeled back to the shelter of the woods whence they had come. The deployment of "E" and "H" had no sooner begun than the whole plateau was swept by converging fire from La Petite Montagne, Glennes, and the Ravin Marion, while artillery searched the road from north to south. "F," attempting to deploy in support behind "H," was forced to withdraw to the shelter of the road till "H" should have gained distance; and "H," mistaking their withdrawal for an abandonment of the attack, began also to recoil from before that withering fire. Then "F," reforming, passed through it, and struggled on to the edge of the ravine. At the same time "B" was passing through the thinning ranks of "E" Company. The losses were bravely taken, but there was never a chance of success, and at dusk, when "B" Company had been drawn back through the smoke from a precarious foothold gained in the bottom of the east-

115

ern valley, the battalion returned to its original positions. About 8 P. M. a message was received stating that the supporting artillery for the attack would not open fire till 7:30; and whether or not it did then open fire no one noticed, nor was any further attack attempted that night. Before dawn the relief by the Third Battalion was effected, and the Second Battalion withdrew with an effective strength of 247 men, or 25 per cent of their original number.

The First Battalion, supposed during this time to be in support position five hundred yards to the rear, found itself in fact engaged upon the right, and so remained during much of the occupation of the front by the Third Battalion. The 153rd Brigade on the left, and the troops beyond them had gained considerable ground toward the Aisne, but the 28th Division, suffering a reverse on the right, had withdrawn under heavy artillery fire till their left reached almost to the crest of the southward slope; and the capture at night of an outpost of "D" Company, holding the right of the battalion, was the first indication that

116

this flank was widely exposed. Then an enemy patrol of some fifteen men stumbled upon the company front. Neither side had warning of the coming collision, and at point-blank range the German boy-officer shouted the order to charge. It was probably not more than a reconnaissance in force, for it left its dead on the field, including its officer, and only the German artillery took revenge for its losses. Yet a soldier of "D," taken prisoner with the outpost and returning after the armistice, reported that he had seen what looked like two regiments of the enemy massed in and about the Ravin, each man armed with four grenades and apparently intending to drive through the First Battalion position and cut off the Second Battalion beyond Merval; but this attack was never delivered. "D" was withdrawn, forming a front to the flank across the grassy plateau, and the battalion here remained, save for its subsequent attacks upon the Ravin, in a very constant drenching of gas.

CHAPTER VI

MERVAL

THE Third Battalion, after two or three days at Sergy, had, on the afternoon of September fourth, been moved forward to the Bois de la Pisotte, and then on to Villesavoye, camping there on the hillside as Divisional Reserve. Here a spectacular little incident was played out in the air. The huge bulk of an observation balloon, attached by cable to a motor-truck, moved down the hill from the south, and had barely passed when an enemy plane appeared high above. The balloon began a cumbersome descent, swaying its head this way and that like some helpless creature attacked; the plane dipped forward in a long nose-dive. On the hilltop to the east a machine-gun opened fire into the air, another to the west, then another, another, and another—the white smoke tentacles of their tracer-bullets meeting and

118

crossing in a lacy canopy against the blue sky over the back of the balloon. Down swept the plane like a diving fish-hawk, down along the path of its own thread-like fire, down and down, sheer through that screen of burning bullets, along the broad back of its victim, then up at a dizzy angle and away, while a sheet of flame and some crumpled wreckage dropped to earth behind it. The enemy attacking planes were very active during all this period, and as many as three Allied observation balloons were seen in flames at a single time.

After dark on the sixth, the Third Battalion moved forward to beyond the northern outskirts of Fismette, where for nearly an hour an enemy bombing-squadron turned the still night into a chaos of noise and flying débris about their heads. Here, about midnight of the eighth-ninth, the same night upon which the 28th Division on the right was relieved by the 62nd French Division, they received orders to proceed to the relief of the Second Battalion at Merval; and, after passing with a number of casualties through some fairly severe shelling on the road, they took over at

dawn—"K" on the left near Le Verdillon, "L"
in the low ground between Merval and Serval,
"I" and "M" along the crest of the ridge facing east. Orders had been initiated for a further advance at dawn in conjunction with the
French on the right, but were not immediately
received by the troops, nor was any advance
upon the right in evidence. "I" and "M" were
ordered to send each a platoon across the open
plateau to take position on the wooded slopes
overlooking the ground north of Fond de Vas,
and to be prepared to support the French left
as soon as their advance should have developed
and passed beyond Glennes. This order, whose
execution it was, in the first instance, contemplated should take place under cover of darkness, was actually carried out between 8 and
9 A. M., and the slopes, though appearing on
the map to afford probable cover, actually afforded none.

As the lieutenant of "M" Company reached
the brink, a wolf-like dog, with a message at his
collar, trotted out from behind a bush, froze
for a startled instant, and then wheeled back at
a run. The platoon, looking in vain for its

promised shelter, moved down the slope in squad rushes; and at once a battery of field artillery opened upon them with direct fire. Men may speak lightly in retrospect of their dislike for "whizz-bangs," but the point-blank fire of field-guns at a target pilloried in the open is an ordeal to wrench men's souls—the swift rush of sound, the instantaneous crash of the explosion, and then the scream of some disemboweled comrade—again and again, and nowhere on earth to turn to for help. The platoon of "M" Company was withdrawn with losses to the sunken road.

The platoon of "I" on the left, with a little better shelter, held on, and, sending word of its condition, was ordered still to hold. No friendly barrage appeared across its front—it had fallen, such as it was, three hours before—nor was there any movement of French troops across the valley; but instead the fire of machine-guns and rifle-grenades grew steadily in intensity upon its position, mixed with overhead bursts of H. E. and occasional long-handled hand-grenades from the scrub to the left, while an interdiction fire of artillery was laid on the plateau behind. After an hour of hopeless self-sacrifice, when their left outpost had been cut off and all either killed or captured, they too withdrew, singly, along the bottom of a little draw across the plateau, their lieutenant carried out in their rear with a bullet through both lungs. So much for the right.

On the left "K" Company, supported by two platoons of "L," having received apparently mistaken orders to attack, advanced at 8:40 P. M., nine hours behind its barrage, in support of an unsuccessful French attack upon Glennes which had ceased, and moved across the open ground toward Revillon. Again from the sunken road to La Petite Montagne machine-guns and artillery burst into action. Few even reached the wire; none crossed it; and, at 4 o'clock, "K" Company withdrew with fifty-two casualties.

The First Battalion, in conjunction with the French attack upon the right, had been attacking the Ravin from the south and west, and, after considerable loss, had established themselves across its wooded southern end. The French, beyond the swell of ground, had

122

gained possession of the bluffs of the Bois de
la Sauix up toward Le Chapon; but the eastern side of the valley was still strongly held by
enemy machine-guns in concealment, sometimes within a few rods of the American rifle-
pits, and was furthermore completely dominated by observation and fire from La Petite
Montagne. Though the distance here was over
2000 meters it had been so well measured by
the enemy that this long range machine-gun
fire was terribly effective; and their mastery
of the air during this fighting gave great accuracy to their artillery. On the night of the
ninth "I" Company established itself in the
southeast horn of the Ravin Marion, and "M"
in the southwest. There was no immediate resistance to this occupation, though the men,
here dug in, remained under a constant fire.

From September tenth to thirteenth there
was no conspicuous movement upon this front.
"M" Company had pushed a combat group
north along its slope to a point a little short of
the Fond de Vas; "L" Company, which had
suffered constantly from artillery fire from
the left rear—and it always was denied, though

not to the conviction of the troops, that this was from friendly artillery—had been moved up into caves and cellars on the Merval ridge. A field-message book of the lieutenant in charge of "L" Company at this time, picked up in the Marais six months later, shows how constant was this difficulty of artillery from the rear:

"September 9th.—2:45. Our artillery is firing within 25 yards of Company Headquarters. Whizz-bangs, and lots of them.

"September 9th.—3:45. Our artillery just dropped a shell 100 yards east of Company Headquarters, in woods where we have a platoon. Shells seem to be coming from west.

"September 9th.—4:55. Our artillery barraged Serval in our rear at 4:50. It is beginning to tell on the men.

"September 9th.—7:45. Our artillery just fired some low trajectory shells from our left in woods 75 yards in front of Company Headquarters. Do try to stop them."

All this may of course have been slander. Though the direction of the front here ran almost northwest it is often possible to mistake the direction of artillery-fire, and, further, a German gun was reported to be found in action well behind the American line. But the opinion of those who lay day after day in those gas-drenched woods amounted to conviction—and it was uncharitable.

The cave of Battalion Headquarters, where by candle-light the surgeons were constantly at work, passed on its daily quota to hospital or burial. A broken stake, driven into the side-wall of the cave and supposed to be a German booby-trap, was guarded day and night by a sentry, and remained as a modern Sword of Damocles. The roadside cavern near regimental headquarters, itself a cavern in the chalky hill, had been hopefully prepared for American occupants by the slow leakage of gas-shells placed within—and not without results.

For dawn of September fourteenth another attack was ordered, again conforming to the left of an advance by the 62nd French Division, and outposts were drawn in prior to the artillery preparation. This opened at 5:15 for half an hour, mixed with an intense indirect fire of machine-guns from the French. The enemy counter-barrage came down at 5:80, lasting, with drum-fire of 88's, 105's, and 150's, almost continuously till eleven. The eastward valley offered a spectacle of unforgettable grandeur. In the earlier darkness some wooden buildings, afire at its mouth, lit a false dawn in the east. Then in the growing light one saw its level meadows cloaked with the mists of morning, and its steep sides shrouded in smoke; they mingled and merged into one vast cauldron of vapor, stabbed through and through with flashes of fire, blotting out the farmsteads beyond, till only La Petite Montagne, floating above a sea of cloud against a blood-red sky of dawn, lifted its smoking, flame-wreathed head like a volcano in eruption; and always through the crash and shock of explosions wove the swift hammer-song of countless machine-guns. Yet slight indeed was the advance effected. "I" Company succeeded in working along the east side of the valley about half its length to a point of contact with the French, who never gained a mastery of Glennes, if indeed they entered it; "M" did no more than resume its former position along the west side. "D" Company occupied the valley-bottom until shelled out of it again to join in an ineffective advance with "A" and "B" in the afternoon. Late that evening Lieutenant Jenkins, in command of "D," upon a self-authorized mission to the French major, succeeded, in probably incomprehensible French and lucid gestures, in effectively directing him to reoccupy the bluffs overlooking Glennes, which he was about to abandon.

"K" Company, with half of "L" in support, started upon an eventful day. Battalion headquarters had been moved back, previous to the bombardment, to a cellar in Merval, where, about 6 A. M., qualified orders were given to "K" and "L" Companies. These were to be prepared to take position for an attack upon Revillon within thirty-five minutes of receipt of word that Glennes had been captured by the French. At 10 A. M. the major of the First Battalion, which was acting in close support of the Third, came forward with an order that the left should be prepared to attack at 9:30. The lieutenant in charge of that part of "L" started down into the Marais Minard with instructions to connect with troops on his right and await the lifting of the barrage in his front. The three succeeding messages he sent back were to the effect that there were neither troops on his right nor a barrage in his front. At about eleven he, together with "K" on his left, attacked.

The enemy resistance was in no way weakened, but after heavy losses they dug in along the wire before the sunken road, the line running southeast and northwest from beyond St. Pierre Ferme to somewhat short of the first crossroad. Here they held during the afternoon and the fighting had seemed to be over for the day, when, at 4:55 P. M., the captain of "K" received word that a barrage would be laid down along the wire and the road at five o'clock. There was no time to protest; there was no time to organize a withdrawal; there was no means of guessing that the barrage would consist of some seven or eight shells which would better have been faced where the companies then were. They streamed back across the meadows, and reorganized under cover for a fresh attack. But this could not be immediately accomplished, and though "M" and "I" of the 308th were thrown in on the left and "C" of the 307th on the right, the attack, when delivered at dusk, was the most costly yet launched over that trampled, blood-soaked way. They cut a way through the wire, wiped out the crews of four machine-guns in the sunken road, and established themselves in a German trench on the near brink of it. "C" was then drawn back into right support; the two companies of the 308th were in support on the left. Five officers had fallen in the two attacks—Lieutenant Felter with a bullet through the forehead as he emptied his gun at the muzzle of a machine-gun in action—and only one officer was left on the front line.

A fresh squad from "L" Company came down from the cave on the ridge, and, without finding the rest of their company or any one who could give them instructions, settled down on the right. The night came down very dark. At eight o'clock an enemy barrage came down on the position, held for twenty minutes, mostly upon the Marais to the rear, and then lifted;

there came the shuffling of feet in the darkness
ahead, a command, hoarse shouting of German
voices, a calling out for Lieutenant Miller,
then a volley of hand-grenades and the American line broke to the left. Lieutenant Miller
was last seen doing his single best to rally it,
and his body was never found. Two chauchat
posts were still in action, firing across the front
from the right, but the sunken road and trench
were again occupied by the enemy. How the
broken troops got back none of them ever knew
—somewhere through or around the 308th.
There was one more attack before dawn when
the Italians, who were now waiting to take
over the sector, insisted upon a trench, no matter where situated, for them to occupy; and
the captain of "K," sweeping together what
troops he could find, filed through the gaps in
the wire, reoccupied the trench beyond with a
shower of hand-grenades, and, turning it over
to the Italians, left them to work out their own
salvation. This was found in an early withdrawal.

The Italians had begun passing that evening through Fismes, where Rear Regimental

Headquarters was located in a cellar. The town was still under fairly constant shell-fire —a dreary place of dust and débris and sun-scorched carrion. The Italians expressed themselves, through interpreters, as dissatisfied with the whole situation; and no one disagreed with them. Yet their escape in the streets of Fismes seemed miraculous. They arrived, about two battalions together, in close column of squads, and met head on with a column of withdrawing French, where, at the bridge between Fismes and Fismette, a motor-truck had broken down across the right of way. On the street where, since the costly crossing of the Second Battalion, no larger body than a platoon had been allowed to congregate, a force of nearly three battalions stood crowded together; where, for fear of drawing shell-fire, never a lighted cigarette-butt had been shown, the place looked like a hay-field filled with fireflies; and, almost stationary, they stood there for seven hours. The American M. P. in charge of road-traffic was faced with a serious problem; and, as neither French nor Italians either understood or followed any of his suggestions, he failed to master it. The interest of Regimental Headquarters was frankly selfish—they wanted the Italians to live long enough to effect the relief, and then they might choose their own way. A little before daylight the Italians won through and continued their firefly-way to the front; and through the whole night a solitary shell exploded near the bridge, and injured only a single mule.

The relief of the front was decidedly complicated. On the night of the 14th-15th, the Second Battalion relieved the First; during the same night the Italians had on the left been persuaded and maneuvered into taking over; elsewhere they expressed a reasonable but untimely wish to reconnoiter. Nothing noticeable occurred during the day, beyond a growing irritation with the Italians, and that night the Second Battalion drew out.

Morning of the sixteenth found "M" and "I" Companies still occupying opposite sides of the unloved valley and adrift in a world of loneliness and foreigners. At intervals a Frenchman, in evident distress, would slide over the bank into the P. C. and gasp out:

"Les Boches! Les Boches!" or a deputation of Italians would, with equal emotion, demand explanation of things that no one knew about in a language which no one understood; and meantime there were being sent hither and thither messengers who seldom found the proper recipient of their message, more seldom returned with a reply, and almost never solved the difficulty referred to. Toward noon the lieutenant in command of "M" Company sent word to the lieutenant in command of "I," asking if he were still there and how he did; and Lieutenant Lord, in command of "I," sent reply: "Battalion Headquarters seems a little incoherent, and our new allies a trifle excitable; but I am having a perfectly good time, and hope you are too. Why worry?"

The message expresses much of the spirit of the American army. After dark of the sixteenth these two companies, having received permission to draw out at their discretion, left the Italians to arrange, after their own manner, their difficulties with themselves and the enemy. The Regiment was assembled, during the sixteenth and seventeenth, some marching, others carried in lorries, half famished and wholly exhausted, in the quiet woods between Arcis le Ponsart and the Abbaye d'Igny, sixteen kilometers to the south.

THE SUNKEN ROAD—MERVAL, SHOWING A LITTER OF AMERICAN EQUIP-
MENT AT THE ROADSIDE—THE DÉBRIS OF THREE ATTACKS

MILESTONES ON THE ROAD TO VICTORY

CHAPTER VII

SHEETS AND BANDAGES

As giving a fair picture of the more cheerful side of hospital experience at this time, some extracts from letters and a diary may here be of slight interest.

"It seemed a long way back. The first part, of course, I walked, but I had swallowed a fair amount of blood and when I added a lungful of gas, in a swampy hollow into which I dropped to get rid of some overhead H. E., it made me sick. As I passed the chalky hilltop of the forward dressing-station four shells burst near the mouth of the cave; so I went on. There is nothing there but a dressing-station, and I don't see why they can't leave it alone. At Les Prés farm Lieutenant Sloane, one of the most cheerful souls on God's earth, dressed the wound, gave me an injection of A. T. S. (anti-tetanus serum) and put me on the front

185

seat of an ambulance for the divisional station at Mareuil-en-Dole.

"Upon arriving at this station they looked over the bandages, and gave me a lot of steaming hot coffee; then on again through Fère-en-Tardenois and, seemingly for hours, through a quiet moonlit country of woods and meadows blanketed in cold mist, to a château and a vast tent filled with loaded stretchers. One was a Boche, wounded somewhere in the back, so that he lay on his face and kept glancing over his shoulders as though expecting to be bayoneted. There was an attractive girl there in a red flannel waist, going round among the wounded—and it seemed as though I hadn't seen one for years. I saw my poor guide there, too, and his arm looked rather bad. He had three bullets through it. I never shall forget seeing him trying to bend it up in a ball and stuff it in his pocket as he ran. He still seemed much more concerned over me than himself.

"The surgeons were desperately busy, but yet seemed to find time for gentleness and kindness and a hearty cheerfulness which wasn't boisterous enough to jar. From time to time an orderly or the girl would come by to ask if I needed blankets or cigarettes or cocoa, or

186

would like to lie down on a stretcher till the ambulance came to take me on.

"During the next ride I had rather lost sense of direction or time, but it was nearly dawn, and bitterly cold, when we reached the Evacuation Hospital at Couin. I was told to undress in a windy tent and waited half an hour, with a blanket round me and my valuables in a little cotton bag at my side, for my turn on the table, so I was shivering like a leaf when I got on. The operating major, a thin, bruskly spoken little man, glanced me over and up and down and then, looking searchingly into my face, as though trying to master my spirit, told me shortly not to be so nervous. It annoyed me and I probably showed it, for next day he lent me his dressing-gown and the use of his tent, with its comfortable armchair, box of cigars, and set of Kipling. We were ranged in cots along both sides of a long ward-tent, and, except for the food and the flies, were very well looked after.

"One doesn't like to complain, but the food was really very poor and insufficient, and the constant swarm of flies about my face-bandages rather exhausting. There were only two fly-nets available for the ward, and they, of course, were wanted for the men who couldn't move their arms. It is the unnecessary hardships that one feels the most, and only they of which one has right to complain. And one is so sure that the people at home wish us, who are in hospital, to be properly fed and, when we need it, to be provided with a few yards of mosquito-netting so that we could lie still. They have sacrificed dearly for such things and much more—and yet it seems that they can't reach us with their sacrifices.

"The 28th Division seemed to be having a bad time around Fismes. All day long officers were coming in on stretchers from the operating room. A Texas major, a great whale of a man, was put in the cot beside me, gloriously drunk with ether. I heard him muttering to himself:

" 'The best looking bunch of Huns I ever seen—them were regular fellows.' Then he lifted a red unshaven face from the pillow to blink at me.

" 'Say,' he whispered confidingly, 'them per-tater-smashers is *great*. I seen three men trying to get out of one window to get rid of one of them fellows.' A pause, while he vomited over the side of the bed, then with a chuckle, 'and they done it, too—I was one of 'em.'

"He dropped back on to the pillow and

made faces at the fly on his nose; then, having made up his mind to brush it off, he stared at his hand for a moment and resumed with sudden earnestness.

" 'I want to tell you about George. George is a damn good kid. One of 'em calls acrost the street, "Was Kompanie ist das?" and George sort of sneezes at him in Dutch while he pulls the string on a pertater-smasher. So the Hun asks it again and George lobs the thing across to him in the dark. Hell of a way to answer a civil question! He must ha' had some friends though, and what they done to us was too much—I wish some one 'ud find George. He's a damn good kid.' Then he dropped off to sleep.

"Some time in the night I heard them carrying in a man to the cot opposite—raving his way out of ether—and I recognized Major Jay's voice:

" 'What's the matter? Oh, you're hurting my arm. . . . All right, Dudley, I'll stay here a bit. Send again and find out. You *must* find out. They can't *all* be gone.'

"It was terribly dramatic, lying there in the darkness and piecing together the story of some dim disaster to my regiment.

"The next day a number of us were carried

by ambulance to Château Thierry, for a barge trip down the Marne to Paris. As we waited on the float I saw Sergeant Parkes of my company carried on—four or five of his ribs crushed in by a shell. He was very pale and in some pain, but I think not severe, and he seemed very glad to see me, holding on to my hand while he spoke. One of the first things he asked was whether he would be sent back to the company again when he got well, and what he must do to make sure of it. I was remembering him in the early days at Upton, when he never seemed to get a uniform to fit him, and how for weeks he drilled the recruits of the Annex Barracks in an old blue serge suit and a campaign hat; and how he came into the orderly room one day with his earnest, respectful manner and slight stammer, to apologize for the fact that his civilian shoes no longer had soles on them. Brave, faithful soul, he died that week in the Paris hospital.

"For those of us who could sit on deck it was a wonderful journey—wrapped in our bandages and blankets in the summer sunshine, watching the green and peaceful country glide by—the sedgy banks where the water-hens paddled about through the rushes, the high slopes of stubble and poppies with their clutch-

es of pheasants, lush meadows of pasturing
cattle, vistas of shiny-leaved sycamores, just
tinting into autumn, and endless lines of tall
poplars. It breathed of a security and quie-
tude whose existence we had forgotten, and it
smelled delicious. In the little villages through
which we passed people thronged down to the
water's edge to watch us with an awed interest—for we were the first to pass that way—
and often one heard the words: *'Ceux sont
les blessés Americains.'* Old men, fishing from
flat-bottomed boats—and French rivers are
lined with old men fishing—stood up with un-
covered heads or at salute as we drifted by;
and at the locks children threw down flowers
to us. One felt very proud of one's place in
that simple pageant, bearing witness through
the land of France that America had indeed
taken her stand beside France's thinning armies on the line. At night we tied up to the
bank beneath the beechwood of an old château,
and the Red Cross girls, who had been circu-
lating through the day with grapes and chocolate and cigarettes, cooked our supper. Then
on at sunrise, winding and winding down to
Charerton, and by ambulance to Number 8
Hospital in Paris, which seemed to me the

most comfortable and desirable spot on earth
—except home."

    *   *   *   *   *

Another story written at somewhat later
date, after bitter fighting in the Argonne
Forest, tells of another aspect of that same
red journey back from the line of battle:

"We had gone only a little way up the slope
when I noticed that something was wrong with
my shoulder, but not much apparently, as
everything I had still seemed to work. I never
felt when the bullet hit me. A few minutes
later I was looking at my map with the battalion commander when something happened
again. There was a sudden film of smoke before my eyes, a sledge-hammer blow across the
knees, a confused sense of lifting, and then I
was down on my face among the leaves. I
heard some one calling out:

" 'The Captain! The Captain! Don't leave
him there. All right, sir, we'll have you out
in a moment.'

"Then I was being dragged along by the
arms, with my feet trailing useless behind, till
we came to the railroad track and a stretcher.
My mind had cleared by that time and I remember giving my legs a try, as I couldn't see

142

a great deal the matter with them; but they seemed to be missing on about three cylinders, and I concluded to call it a day. Four men carried the stretcher, putting the poles on their shoulders, and an officer told me afterward that I looked like some eastern potentate starting on a journey. I seemed to meet every one that I knew along the railroad track, which was cheering, both from their greetings and because my company's attack had looked rather lonely at the time I left. Everything seemed to be coming up, and I was sure they would be needed. The battalion commander passed me, limping along on his enormous stick toward the rear. He said he thought that he could make the grade, and that the Colonel of the 808th had taken over command for the moment, but had sent back for Captain Grant to lead the battalion. A little farther I passed Captain Grant dead on the roadside, and his only lieutenant beside him, dying. The shelling along the valley bottom was getting rather bad, so, as the first aid post looked very busy, we did not stop there. Then I passed my former company drawn up in a side gulch, and Sergeant Watson, who was then in command of it—as they had no officers left, and the First Sergeant had been badly bruised by a shell splinter—Sergeant Watson, as I say, came out and insisted on looking me over before I went on. I remember joking him about the way he never seemed to get hurt—he was so splendid a soldier that one could afford to—and he wrinkled his forehead and answered, rather apologetically, that he didn't know why it was; and then afterward I heard that three days later he was killed.

"He and Durgin were the first sergeants that I had made at Upton. He came to camp in an old brown sweater and little gray cap, wearing his habitual rather worried and cross expression, though in fact he was neither cross nor worried, and I had picked him as a likely-looking man to clean out the wash-house. The place had been turned, in the first afternoon of use, to something like a pigsty struck by lightning, and he had turned it back to the resemblance of a Pullman dining-car. I gave him two men and told him to keep it so, and, as soon as I had heard him give them instructions, added eight more and told him to clean out the barracks. He didn't know a thing about military matters, being a steam-fitter by trade, but he was there to learn, and he was born to command. In those early days one was apt to use one's best material rather selfishly—one had to to keep going—and after keeping the inside of the barrack and wash-house above criticism for a fortnight, while Durgin bossed a gang digging the stumps and collecting and stacking loose lumber in the company area—Watson came to me and said he was afraid of getting behind in the drill. He needn't have been, though.

"I remember one evening when I was lecturing the N. C. O.'s, as one often did after supper, and was speaking of taking direction from the stars. Very few of them claimed to know the North Star by sight, so I was drawing out the Big Dipper on the blackboard, and explaining why two of its six stars were called the Pointers, when Watson raised his hand and respectfully suggested that I was drawing it faced the wrong way. For the life of me I didn't know whether I was or not, but told him I would take his word for it. After that, of course, I had to say something to reëstablish my own reputation for learning, so I touched briefly on the difference between mean-solar and sidereal time, on the traveling of the vernal equinox in right ascension, and on the migration of the isogonic lines. I knew that it couldn't mean a thing to them, and after a few sentences I came back to earth; but Watson

stayed after class was dismissed to find out all
I knew.

"One saw another side of his thoroughness
in Lorraine, where he was Platoon Sergeant of
the First Platoon, and coming late one night
along the line of outposts I found him camped
in one of them. He told me, in open hearing of
the men, that this outpost was always com-
plaining of being sniped at all night, so he
was spending the night with them to see what
it amounted to; he thought that they exagger-
ated. He told me next day that they *had* ex-
aggerated, but probably would not again, and
the relation between morale and exaggeration
works as cause and effect in both directions, so
that it is cumulative.

"Another instance was in the Forest of
Charmes when I noticed the First Platoon bus-
ily policing the underbrush, while the rest of
the Company lay on their backs in the shade.
I asked Watson what it was about, and he told
me that a deputation had represented to him
that the platoon was doing more than its share
of work, always a popular fallacy with all organizations, and had urged that he speak to
me about it. Instead of which he had assembled the platoon, spoken briefly to them, and
then, deploying them in skirmish-line, had with

them policed the entire company area—with the result that the company area was clean, that there was no hard feeling, nor any further complaint from the First Platoon.

"Well, he is dead now, poor fellow. I have spoken of him at such length first, to show what the best material of the draft was like, and second, because I was fond of him. But it is always the best who are killed, and I must get back on my stretcher, for I left myself in a place that was rather unhealthy to linger about in. We stopped again at the Dépôt de Machines, where was the main dressing station, but it was also an important cross-road, and the shells were ranging in on it rather close. The surgeon came out to me on the road, and I had the distraction of watching them while he bandaged my legs and shoulder and face. I might mention that it was a rifle-grenade that got me the second time, and it must have landed nearly at my feet.

"We went on up the tracks in the gathering darkness, and it was interesting to pick up the old familiar landmarks that already seemed so remote. The German blanket and tin of bully-beef that I had thrown away that same day, against my better judgment, but because I had to—they were still lying there, but I

147

shouldn't need them now; the log hut where Gilbert had been so suddenly and mysteriously gassed, and out of which battalion headquarters had been shelled; the little quarry in which we had slept before the attack on the Dépôt; the cemetery where we had eaten breakfast after that rather awful night, when I knelt for an hour in the drenching darkness by poor H—, with my finger on the pulse in his throat, listening to his slow snuffling breath, and waiting for breathing and pulse to cease. His brains were half out over his cheek, and the open grave, with his comrade already in it, was waiting at his feet; and I had time in plenty to think how much it would mean to some unknown woman across the water when they did cease. After that the way was unfamiliar and utterly dark.

"They must have carried me over three miles, stumbling in the black night along the railroad ties of the narrow-gauge line, heartbreaking work for tired and hungry men; but always, when they set me down to rest, a shell would come ranging in, and one or the other would say: 'Well, what do you say? We've got to get the captain out of this.' And so the weary march would be resumed. Some machine-guns were firing from a dark hill-crest beneath which we passed, and I wondered vaguely what they were doing so far behind. Then we came to the near end of the relay-posts and I bade my men good-by, wishing them luck from my heart as they started back for the line. One of the men at the relay-post started to tell me how they had been carrying there all day without food or relief; but the other cut in with:

"'Don't tell that to the captain. He's not here to help you out. You're here to help him.'

"And the first man laughed as he hitched the slings over his shoulders, and said:

"'Well, I guess that's right enough. We'll do the best we can, sir, and I guess every one's doing that to-day. We don't have the worst of it here by a lot.'

"There were three relays of perhaps half a mile each, but the shoulder-slings made it easier for two to carry me than it had been for four of my own men without them. Of course, as a piece of furniture I am rather heavy. Then we came to a flat-car drawn by a horse, which had a way of stopping short on the down grades; and, as I overlapped the stretcher by a foot or so, I would take the whole impetus of the car on my legs against the horse's hindquarters. I tried to persuade the French driver that it wasn't what I liked, but he assured me that the horse was tired. It fell down twice, so I imagine that was true; the war is being fought by such desperately tired men and horses. Three times the car ran off the tracks into the ditch. There were two other men on it beside myself, but only one of us seemed to be badly hurt and he had fainted.

"At last we came out into open country where some ambulances were drawn up. I had almost forgotten that there was anything but forest in the world. The drive might have lasted anywhere from half an hour to a week; it wasn't very rough, and they had covered us well with blankets, but not being able to change one's position came hard after a while. I suppose it was the same night when I found myself in a great cathedral. It stretched away in all directions into the darkness, paved with endless stretchers, and the bases of its huge piers lit with lanterns. Above was darkness, the vague forms of Gothic capitals and interlacing arches, with here and there a ragged gap of sky and the stars shining through. I lay directly beneath the crossing, whose groined vaulting seemed from that position to soar to impossible heights. Here and there groups of faces came out into strong light and black sil-

150

houette about the lanterns on the tables; elsewhere dim figures moved to and fro among the
crowded stretchers. One had a feeling of being part of some magazine illustration, but the
cold was real enough. It was cold as death,
and the stone floor was wet with the night fog.
People kept coming and asking where I was
hurt, and dripping hot candle-grease on my
chin as they looked at me, though they meant
to be helpful. At last a Red Cross man came
over with a cup of hot cocoa and a doughnut,
and that helped a lot; then a little later he returned with another cup, a slab of chocolate,
and a packet of cigarettes, and that seemed to
supply my every earthly want. He told me
I was at La Chalade Field Hospital, and would
go on soon to an Evacuation Hospital; only
the urgent cases got treatment here.

"So in due time on I went to a place where
they looked through me with an X-ray, and
then gave me ether. I have always loathed
ether, but for some reason I didn't mind it
then; and I drifted from it, without ever waking, into twelve hours of natural sleep. When
I did wake it was in a smooth white bed, looking out through an open window at a vision of
sunny foliage and golden evening light, and
oh, the blessed silence of the place; not a ma-

chine-gun to be heard from horizon to horizon.
Then I found a sweet-looking nurse in spot-
less white smiling down at me, and asking if
I were ready to eat. I was very ready. To
sleep and eat, and sleep again, and to listen
to the silence; I asked nothing better of life
than that."

CHAPTER VIII

THE FOREST OF ARGONNE

At dawn of September 17th, the last elements of the Regiment, after a long night march, reached the hilltop above l'Abbaye d'Igny, and fell asleep in the sunny woods; after dark of the same evening the regiment was loaded in motor trucks for the Argonne. The name meant nothing then, only a vast stretch of forest where nothing occurred, and the regiment little dreamed that its immediate task was to alter that meaning. It thought it was going to rest. The St. Mihiel drive had just been brought to brilliant conclusion, and it was satisfactory to know that somewhere things were going well. The morale was good, but the troops were rather discouraged, very ragged, and utterly tired; most of the sergeants were gone, and the companies averaged not more than two officers apiece.

FROM UPTON TO THE MEUSE

The journey by motor trucks was unquali-
fiedly awful. They were desperately crowded
and quite innocent of springs, so that he who
found room to sit felt as though perched upon
a cocktail shaker; and it lasted for sixteen
hours. On the afternoon of the 18th the troops
were unloaded at Le Chatelier and Givrey,
remaining there in wooden barracks until evening of the 19th. That day came word that
the Regiment would move at night, and all baggage, kitchens, and rations, should be dragged
to the cross-roads; at nine P. M. came word
that the regiment would not move, and all
baggage, etc., was to be returned to billets; and
at eleven-ten P. M. came word to move at
eleven-thirty. After some turmoil, and in mis-
anthropic frame of mind, not improved by the
rain, the Regiment started upon its longest
march of thirty-four kilometers. Toward
dawn, when the lameness or laziness of the few
was giving place to the serious exhaustion of
the many, a staff-car passed the head of the
column which had halted for a ten-minutes
rest; and, to those who stood near, it is probably one of the bitterest memories of the war

154

that that staff or field-officer, whoever he may
have been, as he leaned from the window of his
car, could find nothing to say to those tired
men beyond a sharp reprimand that they
should be found smoking at a halt in the rain.
It was long miles behind the line, and the rain
would effectually prevent any aerial observation; yet it seemed to him a good opportunity
for disciplinary authority, and it seemed so to
no one else.

About nine A. M. the battalions, in admit-
tedly ragged formation, drew into Florent.
Here they had just succeeded in billeting themselves and eating all the eggs in town, when
orders came for the battalion and company
commanders of the Second and Third Battalions to proceed at once to the Line of Resistance held by the French four kilometers to
the north. The two battalions were to follow
and effect the relief of the line that night. The
company commanders had never quite acquired
the habit of doing and dying without, at least
privately, reasoning about it, and they now
proceeded, still reasoning, upon their way. By
midnight relief was effected of the rear ele-

ments of the 71st French Division, the Third
Battalion being placed forward on the Line
of Resistance in the Bois des Hauts Batis,
across the Florent-La Placardelle road, west
and a little north of La Chalade, the Second
Battalion two kilometers farther south on the
road, and the First Battalion just north of
Florent. The picket-line, which was in fact
a line of resistance, was still held by the French
along the steep slopes southwest of the Biesme,
opposite the Four de Paris, as was also the
line of outposts, on the lower part of the bleak
ridges across the river. The French thus preserved a screen intended to conceal the arrival
of American troops in their rear; but the sig-
nificance of this was not yet apparent to those
most interested.

September 21st to 23rd was of a calm which,
it became increasingly evident, presaged a
storm. An increment of men was received
from the 40th Division, seventy-two to each
company, excellent material, mostly from
Montana and Nebraska, but largely untrained
and wholly inexperienced, and bringing none
of its greatly needed N. C. O.'s with it. Though

none had apparently ever seen a grenade, and
many seemed never to have fired a rifle, yet
they were healthy-looking, untired, and well-
clothed, which was true of not many of the
others. These men had in fact been inducted
into the service only three months before, and
had spent two of those three months in travel.
They had at least no prejudices to be overcome
and were used to taking care of themselves in
the open. The companies were re-squaded and
reorganized, with provisional appointments to
fill the gaps, but, for the forward companies
at least, no drill or training could be attempted.
The region was thickly wooded and it was ordered that men should be kept at all times well
hidden in the woods. They lived, greatly
crowded, in old log dugouts and shacks; the
manning of the Line of Resistance was, save
for a few sentry-posts, little more than an academic exercise to provide a basis for reports.
It was, and had long been, a very quiet sector;
the dense forest made movement well-nigh impossible for either side, and the lines had remained practically unchanged since the first
autumn of the war. In '16 a German attack

had been flung back across the river, since when the lines had been held with fewer and fewer men; and, beyond the occasional cutting off of an outpost at night or the perfunctory shelling of a cross-road, little had been attempted. It was understood that the German line was deeply and thoroughly organized with machine-gun positions.

The French territorial troops, benign old men looking rather like walruses, who manned the machine-gun positions of the Allied Line of Resistance, and had done so apparently for years, spoke of the war as a background to life rather than as an occupation, and reckoned casualties only by season and by name. The Americans began to feel encouraged and to look forward to growing old beside them in this pleasant sunny forest. Then on the 24th the company commanders were directed to reconnoiter the front.

As seen through a slot-like aperture in an observation post overlooking the Biesme, it seemed quite unalluring, and on closer inspection was even worse. It was a bleak, cruel country of white clay and rock and blasted skeletons of trees, gashed into innumerable trenches, and seared with rusted acres of wire, rising steeply into claw-like ridges and descending into haunted ravines, white as leprosy in the midst of that green forest, a country that had died long ago, and in pain. The closer inspection, made in the disguise of French overcoats and helmets, showed a single bridge across the stream, whose approach-trench, completely enfiladed by the enemy position, bore evidence of direct hits by artillery; and, beyond the disused highroad, and the solitary ruin of the Four de Paris, a labyrinth of approaches and trenches, largely abandoned and blocked with wire, débris and brambles. The many dugouts were also largely blocked with wire and broken cots, while their steps, degenerated into a uniform slide of mud, suggested travel in but a single direction and to a destination quite unknown. The little garrisons of the outposts half way up the slopes, already separated beyond redemption from their friends, sought to achieve a like isolation from their enemies by means of portcullises of barbed wire; but life seemed only possible in the place on a basis of live and let live, which was apparently something of the basis of mutual agreement then reached.

That day the commanders of the units down to and including companies were assembled by the divisional commander and informed that they were about to take part in the greatest offensive yet launched, which should extend from the North Sea to Switzerland, and, it was hoped, would finish the war. Of course it was so hoped, but, by most of the regiment, without exuberant optimism; for the war, as last seen in and about Merval, seemed to require more finishing than did the 807th Infantry.

Then artillery began to arrive. All night long it arrived, crushing and clanking through the underbrush, and in the morning the woods were filled with it, concealed under screens of new-cut leaves. Two hundred guns were massed in the divisional area—the 804th and 805th light artillery, the 806th heavy, and the 802nd heavy trench mortars. In spite of precautions the enemy guessed at attack, though, as was later learned, on no such scale as was being prepared. During the 25th their artil-

lery fire reached a volume such as the forest
had not heard in two years of its peaceful warfare. Aeroplane photographs were distributed, and innumerable maps dealing with a country visionary leagues to the northward. Even
clothing was received, though in large measure
too late to be distributed to the ragged leading
battalion, and a vast supply of unfamiliar grenades and pyrotechnics. As the battalion filed
out at dusk of the 25th, an officer stood at the
roadside explaining their various purposes and
methods of functioning, and expounding, like
a patent-medicine artist at a fair, their many
sterling qualities.

"This one will call down a friendly barrage
in your front; you better take a couple. This
one will indicate your position to a passing
aeroplane, works equally well by day or night,
every soldier should have one (wait till the
plane circles about and drops six white stars).
This will burn through flesh and bone and provide a high quality of illumination for night-
attacks (may be thrown by hand or from the
rifle). And here is one (with apologies for
the fact that it weighs ten pounds) that will

161

destroy man and beast within a radius of forty yards (pressing it into the arms of some bewildered soldier)," and so on till his voice was lost in the darkness.

There was a mile of open road, then a trench dipping steeply down the slope. The French captain in command of the forward troops, a tall splendid-looking man, stood on a side terrace assigning the guides to the companies and half-companies, each on a separate ridge, "M," "L," "K," and "I" from right to left. Then a clasp of hands, a cheery "bonne chance," and so onward, slipping down the muddy trench, over the silent stream, and out into the open road beyond, where the companies split upon their different ways.

"Vous allez attaquer?" whispered the guide at one's elbow, incredulous at this American madness, *"Ici dans l'Argonne?"* From Switzerland to the sea, and God only knew what it might mean.

On the right of the regiment moved the 806th and 805th Infantry, and beyond them, along the edge of the forest the 28th Division. On the left was the 808th Infantry, with the 868th colored Infantry, from the 92nd Division, acting as liaison between the 77th and First French Divisions. A word of explanation may here be inserted pointing the difference between the meanings of the words Argonne and Argonne Forest. The former refers to the whole region between the Aisne and the Meuse, largely open country, though with small patches of woods; while the latter refers to a very dense and continuous woodland some twelve kilometers at its widest point from east to west, and thirty kilometers from north to south. The path of the 28th Division was to carry it free of the forest by the third day's advance, while that of the 77th lay squarely along its major axis from La Harazee to Grand Pré, where was its northern boundary. It is thus worth noting that only the 77th was to fight completely and continuously within the forest, because, in spite of this handicap, it was one of the few divisions that was not relieved during the Argonne campaign. The right of the American sector hinged upon Verdun and the whole sector formed the hinge of the great swinging Allied assault. To use the oft re-

peated simile: if the door could be blown off
its hinges, it would constitute a more effective
entry into German territory than if it were
merely kicked open.

The regimental front, forming the right of
the brigade, included from the mouth of the
Rivau des Courtes Chaussés across the Ravin
Intermediaire, the Rivau des Meurissons, the
Ravin Sec, the Rivau de la Fontaine au Mor-
tier, to the Ravin St. Hubert, a distance of
nearly two kilometers, all of which was to be
spanned by the front of the Third Battalion.
The Second Battalion was to move in support,
the First to remain along the Biesme in reserve. The artillery, after holding for three
and a half hours of drum-fire on the enemy
lines, was to advance one hundred yards in five
minutes thereafter, and the infantry were to
keep within five hundred yards of their rolling
barrage—instructions which recurred somewhat hopelessly to the leaders of units during
the ant-like wanderings of the morrow.

Instructions had been given for a very open-
order advance, and as the direction lay due
north, cutting diagonally across the steep

ON THE EDGE OF THAT DESERT REGION ABOUT VERDUN

ridges, it seemed probable that some merging of units would soon result—an estimate which was amply justified by the event. It was hoped that visual liaison would be established by day-light; but it never was. In the many branching trenches squads and platoons became separated in the darkness, or met head-on in the narrow way where no passing was possible. It was never possible in the regiment to pass an order down a column in single file with any hope of its carrying through—a Polack or some limited intellect would invariably intervene as a non-conductor—and the French guides were on this occasion unusually poor, even for French guides. They disbelieved in attacking in the Argonne Forest, and wished to be out of it before any such thing was started. When the occupation of the front was complete, probably between one and two A. M., runners were sent to report it to Battalion Headquarters; and perhaps half of them succeeded in finding its location, but none succeeded in returning to their companies. So the platoons settled down, isolated in the deep chill dugouts with a few sentries posted, awaiting the zero hour, five-fifty, for their advance. The following description of one company's advance is probably typical of all:

"The bombardment started at two-thirty A. M. with a roar stretching from horizon to horizon, and the upper air grew alive with whistling sounds; on the high ground in front the shock of explosions merged into one deep concussion that rocked the walls of the dugouts. The night was thick with mist and bitterly cold —a pale thread of moon gliding and disappearing amidst the moving vapor, the lurid glare flickering up and down along the front. As the night dragged on the mist thickened, wrapping the world in its blind, cold blanket, and blotting out the last stark tree-stump ahead. Orders had been given before leaving camp for a very open-order advance, and there was no chance of getting word to the troops to change the formation no matter what the weather was. So at five-fifty I climbed out with the nearest platoon into darkness and impenetrable fog mixed with powder-smoke, started them forward by compass, and went to look, or feel, for the others. I didn't find them again until afternoon. Our artillery was supposed to have blown a passage through the

heaviest wire between some craters marked
on the map near the head of the Ravin Sec,
but there didn't seem much chance of finding
it by sense of touch. The heavy fog had kept
the powder smoke down, and as morning began to lighten I found myself, with my striker
and two runners, adrift in a blind world of
whiteness and noise, groping over something
like the surface of the moon. One literally
could not see two yards, and everywhere the
ground rose into bare pinnacles and ridges, or
descended into bottomless chasms, half filled
with rusted tangles of wire. Deep, half-ruined
trenches appeared without system or sequence,
usually impossible of crossing, bare splintered
trees, occasional derelict skeletons of men,
thickets of gorse, and everywhere the piles of
rusted wire. It looked as though it had taken
root there among the iron chevaux-de-frise and
had grown; and it was so heavy that only
the longest-handled cutters would bite through
it.

"There seemed to be very little rifle-fire going on and the shelling was still almost all in
front and growing more distant. I remember
trying to light a pipe, but the tobacco was so
saturated with powder-smoke and gas that it
was impossible. At the end of an hour's time

I had collected two squads of infantry with a few engineers, and together we steered on by compass over the seemingly limitless desolation. About nine o'clock we heard voices in a draw beside us, and, taking a chance, I hailed them. They proved to be a platoon and a half of my company with one of my lieutenants, and I was never so glad to see any one in my life. In another hour we had picked up the other lieutenant and something more than another platoon. I figured that we had gone nearly a mile forward without meeting any Germans save two or three killed by shells; the fog was as blind as ever, and we hadn't an idea of what was happening on the ridges to either flank; I knew we were too far to eastward but didn't want to leave the high ground until we could see something.

"We had got beyond the bare moon-country into a dense forest of undergrowth, and were working out the very recently occupied trenches and boyaus when, about noon, the mist suddenly rolled up. There appeared first a deep valley to the west, then a farther slope of brush with scattering pine trees, the sun shining on their wet tops, and finally the wooded ridge to southward from which we had come. Two contact-planes were flying low over the ridges to the west, but except for the whirr of their motors and some very distant shelling there was now no sound, nor could I see any sign of other troops. It was not one's idea of a battle; several of the men had already dropped asleep in the bushes. In the opposite slope, and a little behind us, a cul-de-sac, with some wooden shacks in it and a little cemetery, looked like the Fontaine la Mitte on the east boundary of our regimental sector and promised developments; so we slipped and slid down to the valley bottom and were met with automatic rifle-fire from the farther crest. We were able to outflank them on both sides, though, and they didn't make much of a stand. I told Lieutenant Rogers to try out our new model thermite rifle-grenades on them, but nothing occurred, and I didn't discover till long afterward that the detonators came in separate boxes.

"The sound of our rifle-fire had brought up a wandering half of 'E' Company, so with forces joined we pushed on into the thickest jungle I have ever seen, and it seemed to go on forever. Then came a boyau with some deserted machine-gun positions—the guns and tripods still in place, and three or four sets of body-armor, a straight disused road, a further jungle almost impenetrable, and a sudden burst of rifle and machine-gun fire on our right flank. One man fell at the edge of the road and as two others lifted him out they were each shot, one of them through the heart, and the wounded man was struck again through the body. The map showed an ominous dark blue semi-circle on our right, called the Tr. de Prilep, and though we had almost reached its northern end there was considerable wire about it and apparently a number of guns, so that it did not seem wise to try to force its flank without some knowledge of the rest of the regiment. Afternoon was turning to clear evening with a growing sound of infantry fire off to the southwest, as we took up a position for the night, buried our two dead, and started our wounded back with a runner to search for Battalion Headquarters and report our location.

"Two stray elements from companies of the 806th came up, attracted by our occasional fire, and, though my third platoon was still somewhere at large, we were building up quite a fighting force in front of the Tranchée de Prilep (Tr. des Fontaines), when our runner returned with one from Battalion Headquarters he had chanced into, bringing a verbal order for me to report there with my company. It sounded like a mistake, but one couldn't risk refusing it, so we started back; and in a deep trench, beyond the Fontaine la Mitte, we ran into what looked like a whole battalion of the 808th. What they, who belonged on our left, were doing on the extreme right of our regimental sector I am sure they couldn't have told, but as we were trying to crowd past them the Boche opened with whiz-bangs directly on the spot, getting four of my men, so we didn't stop to ask.

"By now it was black night, and my guide confided the news that, though he knew where Battalion Headquarters was, he didn't know how to get there. It reminded me of the lost Indian who said: 'Indian not lost. Indian here. Wigwam lost.' Only now it seemed probable that both the wigwam and the Indian were lost, together with most of the tribe. My conversation with the guide did not assist me to any idea of 'where it was,' though he still had confidence in his knowledge of it; and by one o'clock, in a fifteen-foot trench, with unscalable walls of mud and a stream along its bottom, I knew where nothing was except the guide, my company headquarters, and half a platoon. It rained all night and we slept in the stream."

A field-message from one of the captains of the Second Battalion suggests more concisely something of the same story:

"26th September, 9:30 A. M. Presume I am at 295.9-270.3. Have touch with only one platoon. Am trying to get liaison with 308th on left, also to the front. Have just found 'K' Company, that is, Lieutenant Pool is here with nine men. Rest are lost. Grant."

It was on the second day that a message was sent forward from the colonel to the C. O., Second Battalion, saying:

"I have a direct order to reach intermediary objective today at 95.3-74.8, 96.6-74.7."

Pure optimism, be it most respectfully said. That row of innocent-looking figures represented the ridge beyond the Dépôt-de-Machines, of which more hereafter, and the order was not, could not be, fulfilled. There was in fact very little advance at all upon that day, which was largely spent in collecting lost fragments and reorganizing for advance upon the 28th. The Second and Third Battalions were to some extent merged under the joint com-

172

mand of Major M'Kinney, who had very recently joined the regiment, and of Captain Blagden, and so remained during the succeeding days. The regimental front had in general reached the southern side of the Ravin Sec (not that of the same name previously mentioned) stretching from the Rivau de la Fontaine aux Charmes to the Tranchée des Fontaines.

CHAPTER IX

THE DÉPÔT DE MACHINES

AT dawn of the 28th, the two battalions, with "M," "K," and "I" across the front, took up their slow and groping progress across the ridges. A more difficult country for an infantry advance, or one better suited to delaying rear-guard action, it would be hardly possible to find. The ridges were cloaked in a dense growth of small trees and the bottoms choked with underbrush; it was seldom possible to see over twenty yards, often not five; the keeping of direction and of contact was a problem new with every moment, and each opening through the leafy wall was a death trap. There was rifle fire from across the narrow valleys—it needed but a few men to do it, well hidden in chosen spots, and looking for a glimpse of khaki among the green, or the shaking of bushes; there were bursts of automatic-fire down

174

the narrow lanes—if the gun had been sighted already, the sound of crashing progress was target enough; there was the slow steady drain of casualties, with never a blow to be struck in return, and oh, the long weary way those wounded had to travel back.

The Tranchée des Fontaines, lying almost wholly in the sector of the 806th, was refused on the right, and it held; so that "E" Company, charged with maintaining liaison with this organization, cheerfully attempted the impossible, and stretched itself across the whole distance of this opening flank. By nightfall "I" Company, running into strong resistance in the gulch leading north to the Dépôt de Machines, had withdrawn from its dead to a little quarry by the roadside; "L" Company, on the brink of the gulch six hundred yards to the east, had met the fire of heavy machine-guns, and made its midnight, groping, burials in the rain. The other companies lay where darkness had overtaken them, ignorant of their own or of each other's positions, "E" Company stretched out in a series of cossack-posts across the whole three kilometers of the day's advance. It was a ghastly night of uncertainty and sudden alarms, of bursts of fire coming from none could say where, of hunger, and of long, long hours of drenching darkness:

"Morning brought a flood of relief and of thrice welcome sunshine. We had lost all contact about sundown, when a sudden burst of shelling close on our rear had hurried us forward; our patrols at dusk down the valleys to southeast and northeast had found nothing but sniping and machine-gun fire, and the fire which) had struck the head of our company came from the west. We had passed the night with outposts to every point of the compass, believing ourselves alone in the wilderness, but with the first hour of daylight we found four other companies within a radius of as many hundred yards. Then came word of rations somewhere down the narrow-gauge line by the Pavillion de Bagatelle, the first, save what we had carried, for three days and four nights. By dint of struggle we got ten sacks, and, as the company was supposed to be in the support line, withdrew some five hundred yards to the little high-walled German cemetery. Its enclosure was a glorious oasis of flowers—roses, blue larkspur, yellow and white blossoming

176

shrubbery—and we sat in sunshine on the brick walks amidst rain-drenched grassy graves and flowers, and ate, and smoked, and felt again the joy of living. Whatever had been or was to come, here at least was peace and beauty, sunshine and food."

On the 29th, little or no progress was made, save on the right where "E" Company, stretched far beyond the breaking point, had abandoned the open flank and pushed to the front, across the head of the east and west valley, to the cross-roads southeast of Les Quatre Chênes. Here, with "M" and "H" in support, it lay face to face with a group of machine-gun nests, which it had tried in vain to outflank from either side. The Machine-Gun Company gave supporting indirect fire from behind the Fontaine-aux-Batons, their bullets clearing the heads of "M" Company by a margin of some fifteen feet and spattering along the road in their front. It was an example of extreme efficiency in fire, but was yet not enough to overcome the enemy resistance. The German efficiency was shown by a direct artillery hit upon one of the American machine-guns.

On the left, the 808th reported their forward battalion in the neighborhood of the cross-roads northeast of the Boyau des Cuistots; but it was cut off from the rest of the regiment, their Lieutenant-Colonel being killed by machine-gun fire in an effort to join it. The whole slope of timber south and southwest from the Dépôt de Machines seemed to be filled with machine-guns, and the long east and west ridge to the north of it was lined with them. The two combined battalions of the 807th faced north and west upon these two fronts with their right flank neglected and open, and with forward battalion headquarters, as usual upon the outpost line, in a log hut halfway between the cemetery and the Dépôt, its open door facing the fire.

From the left came the sound of "I" Company's chauchat teams, trying in vain to force the slope, and their casualties came back in a slow but steady stream; in the northeast was the sound of something like a pitched battle round Les Quatre Chênes, a message from the lieutenant in command of "E" reporting cheerfully that he was in close touch with the enemy;

178

a German plane passed over, skimming the tree-tops, and then their artillery opened. With uncanny intelligence it searched the slope for the log hut, whose walls shook with each nearing explosion, and they were not such walls as one would have chosen for the occasion. As one spoke, every sentence was cut in half by the incoming shriek and crash. Out on the plateau to eastward there spread a thick blanket of smoke, lit toward evening by the red flare of explosions, and through which dim figures of men loomed and disappeared as the supporting companies were withdrawn in search of shelter. Night brought a slackening of fire, but no change in the situation.

By afternoon of the 80th, it was evident that the enemy position was being evacuated, and the two battalions were deployed in double line for a concerted assault behind half an hour's artillery preparation. This artillery preparation had frankly become a thing to dread. There was no direct observation of their fire, due to the blind character of the country and the still apparent lack of aeroplanes; nor was there any direct communication from the

infantry units to the batteries. If a platoon
or company were suffering from the fire of
their own guns, they could send a runner with
a message to that effect to Battalion Headquarters, perhaps half a mile or more distant
through the woods; and Battalion Headquarters, if their wires had not been blown out,
would communicate with regimental headquarters, who in turn would take it up with the artillery; and the artillery would quite likely reply that the infantry were mistaking enemy
fire for their own. Of course, a more reasonable course for the infantry unit was to move
out, provided that this could be done. But
what was also probably a fruitful cause of
trouble was an almost criminal inexactness on
the part of very many infantry officers in map
reading. The terrain was undoubtedly difficult for the attainment of this exactness and
of certainty; but that alone would not sufficiently account for the mistakes made. It was
the one salient point on which the training of
infantry officers was found to be deficient.
Many a company commander or liaison officer
was entirely capable of waving a vague finger

over a valley marked on the map, while stating that the troops in question were "on that hill"; and, if pressed to be more precise, he would give as their coördinates figures which represented a point neither in the valley to which he was pointing nor on the hill on which they were. Another technical difficulty which may or may not have led to misunderstanding, but which certainly seems capable of doing so, was that infantry and artillery officers were actually taught quite dissimilar methods of representing a given point on the map by coördinates.

Be all this as it may, at four P. M. of September 30th it was known to a sufficient number of officers just where the barrage line was to fall; and there the greater part of it fell, but not all. A company of the second line had just posted its right platoon with its head resting on a group of birch trees, when the barrage came down three hundred yards in front, all save one gun, which made hit after hit on the birch trees. The platoon recoiled, shaken and lacking its sergeant, and the gun ranged forward into the center of the front line com-

181

pany. "E" Company, still playing out of luck, received no word of the coming barrage, which fell entirely behind it, so that it was, for the time being, surrounded on three sides by enemy machine-guns and on the fourth by its own artillery fire.

When the artillery ceased, and the infantry went forward, the enemy position was found to have been abandoned, but abandoned with a haste which had found no time for the removal of all the machine-guns from the farther crest, nor of the large stores of material along the railroad. Some of this had been loaded on hand-cars and these left upon the rails, while a few prisoners were captured of those who had too long delayed their withdrawal. Undoubtedly, for all its damage inflicted, the artillery had saved the infantry from far heavier loss at the hands of the enemy. The left of the Regiment had reached and passed the Dépôt de Machines; beyond it the 308th was also in position across the valley; and, although the right of the Regiment was still in the air, at a farther point the 305th had gained considerable ground. For some in the support companies it was a night of strange luxury in the German bungalows, with their elaborate white-birch balconies, and their comfort of cots, blankets, and stoves, of strange pink bread, tasting of malt, and of apple jam.

At early dawn of October 1st, the advance was resumed, though now leading to the west of north, and with the right flank as open as the sea. On the left of the brigade the activities of the 368th were said to have produced somewhat the same situation there. There was the usual rear-guard delaying action, and by evening, after one and a half kilometer's slow advance, the leading elements had encountered another position of organized resistance along the ridge south of the Bois de la Buironne. It was fronted with strong wire and heavy machine-guns, and was not attacked in force on that day. The attack of the next day can perhaps best be typified at first hand.

"Our company lay in right support across the road north of Les 4 Chênes, facing what was actually a No Man's Land to the northeast. There had been during the evening some Stokes' mortar preparation on a position in front, and the companies had all been somewhat withdrawn for it, though it had produced no noticeable effect. At three A. M. Captain Blagden came into the old German dugout where I had been sleeping to tell me that we were to attack behind a rolling barrage on the left front at six, and I remember that my teeth were chattering so with cold that I could hardly answer him. A ration party brought up some stew and coffee from the Dépôt before we started, but not enough for every man to have some of both. They rose, shaking with cold, from the half-frozen mud of an old trench and stumbled numbly forward through a forest white with frost. There was a blind kilometer to go through darkness and dense undergrowth to our appointed position on the line of the coming barrage, and little enough chance for checking up on that position, for we met no other troops. It was as ticklish a piece of map memorizing and topography reading as one would wish; after which we waited for the artillery to tell us if I had guessed it right. It was a relief when the first shells pitched in a hundred yards ahead. We crossed a flat ridge of open timber, whose leaves had all turned yellow over night, the sunrise gilding the treetops. Our artillery was enough to encourage

an advance, but certainly not to destroy any wire; from somewhere in front came occasional bursts of machine-gun fire and the sound of bullets striking the tree-trunks around us. Then came a down-slope of thick brush to a muddy ravine running off to the left, and a farther steep slope with wire. The shelling seemed not to have touched it at all; but neither, fortunately, was it swept by the enemy fire which all passed overhead. We were cutting our way rather cautiously through this when we met with 'H' Company on higher ground to our right, and knew that we were with the Battalion again. Beyond their right 'E' Company was almost abreast, though we did not then know it, for the north and south wagon road between was swept by a machine-gun fire which prevented any efforts at communication. A message at this time from its C.O. is fairly graphic:

"295.95-275.45. Am on this line and Boche is putting *minnenwerfers* on us. M.G.'s still in position and one is at bend of road ahead. Have tried to flank him every way, but he is covered by other guns and it is hard to see in this brush. Can't locate guns close enough to get them with Stokes and think artillery had

185

better be put on them. But if so let us know in time to withdraw, as it has a habit of hitting us."

The other companies had been last heard of near the horse-shed that served as Battalion Headquarters, and of what they might have done since then we knew nothing. Some of the enemy fire seemed to come from overhead among the big beech trees in front, but most of their machine-guns were apparently to the right and had effectively prevented any cutting of the wire there. The sniping was rather serious so that, to reduce casualties, I moved my first and second platoons back across the ridge into support, and put the others into a narrow trench beyond the wire.

A runner came over from the 308th, somewhere on our left, having had to circle far back to reach us, and I was trying to find out from him, on a map which he didn't understand, where they were, when we got an order to attack. A barrage would open at twelve-ten and play for twenty minutes on the ridge in front, after which all front-line companies would as-

THE DÉPÔT DE MACHINES

sault together, and the 808th would assault simultaneously on our left. If only one could
believe it! There seemed not a chance that the
artillery would destroy the wire before our center and right, without which neither "H" nor
"E" could advance; the runner from the 808th
shared my doubts that his regiment expected
any immediate move; the support companies,
and we did not know what their orders were,
were beyond the ridge half a mile to the rear,
and two of my platoons with them; it was already after twelve. I sent back a runner, a
red-headed Irishman named Patrick Gilligan,
to hurry forward my rear platoons, and had
just gotten word to the others to be ready for
an instant advance in open order, when the
shelling started. Nothing semed to be falling
short, but it was all beyond the wire of the
center and right, and we moved forward from
our trench to the edge of the barrage line, a
brigade attack consisting of two lonely platoons. I was thinking of the letter of a would-
be suicide once published in the papers ending:
"Good-by, old world, good-by," and I wondered whether my men realized what they were

187

up against. The barrage was stunning to watch for those twenty minutes, there within forty yards of it—the thick smoke among the leaves, the black fountains of earth, and the great yellow trees crashing down in front. Then it ceased, and at once the whole forest began to echo with a sound like a hundred pneumatic riveters at work. We moved forward into a close wall of foliage, combed and re-combed by the traversing bullets, and we fired blindly into the leaves as we went. The noise was deafening, and I could hear "H" and "E" going into action on our right rear, but nothing from the left. Then Gilligan came up with the other two platoons and saluted with a grin. I told him that I had thought he was lost or headed home, though in reality I didn't see how they had come so quickly nor found me so directly.

"Never fear, Captain," he answered, "and praise God it's here that we are and in time for it all, and yourself so safe." And even as he spoke he was down with a bullet through the brain. I think he was the first to be killed.

We were now on the broad top of the ridge

and were beginning a turning movement to the right in the hope of rolling up the enemy line from west to east, if only the rest of the battalion front could do something through their wire. I sent Lieutenant Rogers with the two new platoons to extend our left in search of the 308th, wherever they might be, and to carry on the enveloping movement. We were facing now nearly east in a wide curve, and it became increasingly hard to preserve direction. When I reached the extreme left of the line I found it well over the farther slope and firing dangerously close to our right; but as I took a man by the shoulders to change his aim, he caught a message from the man beside him and passed it on: "Fire more to the right."

Later I found that the message had been started by the lieutenant with the right platoon to prevent its firing on our left, and is the only instance I know of a verbal message passed successfully and without change down a whole company—which it was never meant to do.

We were widely through the enemy line, but

with our left and rear open to the whole of Germany; yet, if we had only known, that left was within four hundred yards of the position taken up that evening by the "Surrounded Battalion" of the 808th, which had not yet made its historic advance. There seemed no longer anything to prevent the progress of our left to the north, an opportunity which it then appeared useless madness to seize, but for which, later, scores of lives were sacrificed. The position we were attacking lay to the east, and already we were completely separated from our battalion. So to the east our left swung, broke through a narrow belt of wire, and came face to face with the first of the enemy—a huddled group of fifteen men with four light machine-guns, who had been driven from position by the artillery barrage and startled into surrender by the sudden appearance of our men. They were sent to the rear with a guard of four, and I had moved back to our center when there came a hoarse shouting from in front, and cries of *"Kamerad, kommen Sie hier."* My best sergeant, an Englishman, was starting toward them, where we could see their

190

helmets among the leaves, and I shouted to him to stay where he was and shoot.

"It's all right, sir," he answered, turning. "They're most hanxious to surrender;" and then pitched forward on his face, and I emptied my pistol over him with, I hope, some effect. Three other Germans came out on the left, empty-handed and calling: "*Kommen Sie hier;*" then dropped to the ground as a machine-gun opened fire above them. Some one was shooting at them, but I don't know with what result. I went over to the sergeant, who was bleeding, but not very fast, from a wound in the thigh. He asked for a drink of water and died as I gave it to him; I never knew why. A new machine-gun had opened down a narrow lane ahead, showing a close wake of bullets through the long grass, and listening to the right front I found that from the rest of the battalion the fire had ceased. We had broken their line but we seemed to be facing them alone, and there might be heavy wire in front. A further advance would mean a sweeping victory or annihilation. We desperately wanted support for our flank and rear. I

191

reached for the message book in my pocket, and, as I did so, caught sight of some more helmets moving across our front from left to right. At first I thought it was our left platoon that had lost direction, till one showed its steep German sides, and then I forgot the message book.

At about that time a runner brought me a written order to withdraw and prepare to receive a counter-attack, and so that ended it; though it took nearly an hour, beginning at the left, to roll up and collect our whole line. The fourth platoon on the right we never did find, though the lieutenant and I walked over the ground on which we had left it shouting ourselves hoarse; so we concluded it had dropped back down the slope to the left, and two hours later its runner reported to me at the mouth of our old dugout to ask whether it was to dig in where it was, a few rods forward of where we had been and alone in Germany.

Neither "H" nor "E" had succeeded in penetrating the wire in their fronts, though the latter had lost some half-dozen men in the attempt. "H" and "L" each lost over twenty.

Due to the complete lack of warning, the support companies, which, if thrown in behind "L," might well have turned the scale to victory and saved the five subsequent days of bloody struggle for that ground, did not arrive until the attack and withdrawal had been completed, and some of them not until dark. By dint of dropping back half a kilometer to cross the wagon road, "E" now came up on the right of "H." These companies were sufficiently protected from surprise by the wire in their front, and on the left, "L," in the trench beyond the wire, threw forward sentry-squads into the brush; but no counter-attack was delivered.

Through the night there were sounds of activity upon the ridge, though the companies on the line, knowing nothing of the advance of the 308th, accomplished that evening along the ravine to their left, could not guess that they listened to the closing of the gate behind them. With the morning a field-gun went into action on the ridge at some three hundred yards' distance, searching the slope behind the line with direct fire and bursting its overhead H. E.

above the lip of the trench. In that trench, shoulder deep and too narrow to admit of passing, the bursts of four shells caused casualties to men lying prone along its bottom; and even for those who were not struck the sound of its point-blank discharges was unnerving. A carrying detail started back for ammunition, and, though they had been warned to keep off the trail behind the solitary dugout, they had scarcely started before there came a burst of machine-gun fire and then a calling for help. Five were down; and as a lieutenant reached out from the bushes to pull one back under cover a bullet broke the skin across his knuckles and another cut from side to side through the gas-mask strapped to his chest. The day was spent in opening covered routes of communication and in attempting more exactly to locate the machine-gun positions. At dusk a relief of the front was made by the supporting companies, and, though this coincided with a suddenly increased activity of enemy artillery upon the line, there was no further immediate loss.

CHAPTER X

THE SURROUNDED BATTALION

THE night of October 3rd saw the Second and Third Battalions widely scattered. "L" dropped back into battalion support on the right to find evidence of enemy occupation of that ground since their departure before dawn of the second. There was sniping fire all down that flank during the night, a light machine-gun raking the road before the battalion headquarters' horse shed, and sounds as of a pitched battle off to the right rear, where the 153rd seemed to be in difficulties.

The amount of enemy initiative and efficiency displayed by this infiltration of small groups of light machine-gunners and snipers, apparently independent of officers, into the gap between the two brigades, is worthy of note and considerable admiration. In the opinion of the writer it is doubtful whether many of the

American troops, in spite of all that has been written about their acquiring the art and skill of the Red Indian in forest warfare, could have been counted on to do as well.

For the discovery of a gap in a hostile line, the percolation through it, in small and isolated groups, to a depth of over a kilometer, harassing an open flank while the harassing is good, and then at the last moment skillfully withdrawing to one's own lines, all represent a grasp of the general situation, a knowledge of the terrain, and a self-confidence of individuals which are not easily come by.

To return, however, to the disposition of the companies. "M," together with "I" and "F" combined, had been ordered up in support of the attack of October 2nd, but had arrived too late—"M" shortly after the withdrawal, but "I" and "F," guided into a maze of wire down the slope to the west, never reaching the ground at all. They returned to Battalion Headquarters after midnight and were directed, after getting a hot meal at the company kitchens near the Dépôt de Machines, to proceed two and a half kilometers up the railroad track of the north and south valley, and to extend the right of a position in the cross valley, east of the Moulin de Charlevaux, just taken up by five companies of the 308th. Starting again about three A. M. of the third, they met "M" Company, ordered on the same mission, in one of the side valleys to the right, and together they pushed on.

"K" Company, advancing before them, had been guided up the line of the 308th runner-posts across the western foot of the ridge, and was already in position on the right of that now famous ground; but "I" and "M," proceeding without guides up the railroad tracks to the left of the stream, and never finding the line of runner-posts, which had perhaps already ceased to exist, were met at gray dawn with a sweeping fire from the open mouth of the valley, and recoiled for shelter into a side draw to the right. The door was closed which it should nearly wreck the brigade to reopen.

The First Battalion had, on the night of the third, taken over the front, and by noon of the fourth "E," "G," "H," and "L" were grouped in Divisional Reserve about the Dépôt de Machines. They had had one splendid cooked meal, the first in nine days, and were for the most part washing in the muddy little stream and removing the surplus population of their clothes, when orders came for them to report for duty to the Colonel of the 308th north along the railroad. By three o'clock they were massed along the draw running east from the Moulin de l'Homme Mort, and half an hour later "G" and "L" were launched in assault up the north valley. Somewhere in front a battalion of the 308th was cut off, but few if any of the company commanders knew where. "G" advanced with a platoon in skirmish line through the swamp along the line of the stream, "L" a little to the rear along the tracks. So they pased the more open part of the valley to where it narrows and bends farther to the north; they came under a fire from both flanks and the front, and they looked at the work before them—a steep and narrow ravine, its sides choked with brush and wire, the crests to right and left held with machine-guns, rifle- and hand-grenades, a long-distance machine-gun fire sweeping down its length from the north,

198

and the first ranging shells wailing in from across the hills. Roncesvalles or Thermopylæ may have looked so to their assaulting columns,

grim in the sunset light; and the thought rose unbidden to the mind—what a place chosen for men to die.

"G" halted under fire across the swamp, and

"L," as directed by Colonel Stacey of the 308th, assaulted the heights to the left under a fire from their front, right, and rear. There was no artillery preparation other than of counter-battery fire. By dusk they had reached the crest of the plateau, but with the loss of the battalion commander, all three of their company officers, and an unknown number of their men. Lieutenant Rogers, the last of the three to be hit, had crawled forward alone some two hundred yards along a shallow ditch, in an effort to locate the enemy machine-guns, and in so doing had passed over the bodies of two others who had apparently died in the same endeavor. Within thirty yards of a machine-gun in action his knee was half shot away by a sniper even nearer to himself; and under this point-blank fire he managed to free himself from his pack, get a tourniquet on his leg, and crawl backward to the company, which he outposted and put in position for defense. A lieutenant from the 308th was then put in command of the company, but was in turn wounded by morning. Captain Grant of "H" Company, being after the first half-hour the senior officer left in the battalion, started forward to assume command of it, but, before reaching the front, was killed upon the railroad track by a shell, which also mortally wounded his only lieutenant. Lieutenant Jenkins, in command of "E" Company, found himself also in command of the Second Battalion, and almost its only officer, together with, at least temporarily, such elements of the 308th as were on that ground. A precarious footing had been gained on the edge of the western plateau, facing a strong line of wire and trenches to the north, and almost all available reserves had been already engaged. During the night the troops huddled into such shelter as they could find, while the enemy artillery blasted the valley from end to end.

Toward noon of October 5th the brigade commander, coming up on the ground, found the troops withdrawing from a seemingly hopeless position upon the left, and ordered another general assault along both sides of the valley. The companies and battalions were by now thinned and merged beyond definition. New lieutenants, coming up from the rear as replacements, were put in charge of whatever elements were at hand and launched upon whatever attack was under way. Few who took part in those continuous assaults can give any consecutive account of them. Officers returned wounded to hospital never knowing with what troops they had fought, and the men moved to obey their orders half-drugged with exhaustion.

The attack on the east of the valley ran foul of the acres of wire where "I" and "F" had vainly struggled two nights previous, and it got no further. That on the west regained their former positions, but could not better them. The main hope lay in an infiltration up the track, where a platoon of "E" was sent, crawling in single file along the ditch. When the last had disappeared around a slight bend in the way, the battalion commander followed to watch their progress. They all lay in sight of him, and one was yet alive, shot through the legs and returning with his rifle the fire of a machine-gun in position upon the tracks, till another burst of fire from it tore him to pieces. So the attack failed.

202

THE SURROUNDED BATTALION

On the sixth it was reported that the French would attack from Binarville, and another attack was ordered upon the western plateau in conjunction with them. The American attack was delivered, though that of the French seems never to have developed; nor was a yard of ground there gained. There was no further attack upon the left. The story of the right is that of the First Battalion.

The First Battalion, which, after the launching of the First Army Corps offensive at dawn of September 26th, had been moved up in Divisional Reserve to the former French front line facing the Biesme, had on October 1st been shifted again forward but to the west of La Harazee. It was reported that the 368th Regiment of colored troops, acting in liaison between the 77th Division, the left of the First Corps, and the 88th French Corps to its left, had fallen back, leaving a gap between the two. Thus the First Battalion found itself far to the left of its two leading battalions in the Tranchée de Breslau and Tranchée de Magdeburg, the former German front line, in position to stop a possible danger at this point. On the morning of the third the Battalion started forward to the Dépôt de Machines, then in the hands of the regiment, and that night effected the relief of the front, "D" and "C" from right to left on the line, "B" and "A" in support.

The next day they went forward in their first attack, "D" providing a holding fire on the right, while "C" threw a platoon and a half through the wire on the left; but there was little result save a heavy toll of casualties, and by nightfall of the fourth their lines had not been advanced. On the fifth, after a two hours' artillery preparation beginning at noon, the battalion again attacked, "C" and "D" in the front as before, and again was thrown back with heavy loss. The story of the right now also becomes confused. The field messages are largely undated, while in others the dates or map coördinates are seemingly mistaken. Yet the substance of these messages will serve to outline the picture.

"Lieutenant Kenyon ('A' Company) having trouble on right with M. G. in valley. We are filtering forward. Hastings ('D' Company)."

"Have developed a Boche post at 95.7-75.8 and M. G. at 96.1-75.7. We are getting M. G. fire from ravine on our right front. Just lost 4 men from it. Am trying to envelop. Tillman ('B' Company).

"M. G. fire from junction of creeks and in front. Been following wire which goes down slope to north. 'D' to push forward, and think they will get it strong.

" 'D' slowly moving forward, pushing out small combat groups and coming up to them. Seem to have run into an organized position on their right front. M. G. and rifle-fire from front and right. Whiz-bangs on 'D' and 'A.' Hastings has sent for one pounder and is placing Stokes. Tillman has sent patrols to locate 306th.

"Wire is 80 feet thick in places. Have cut through at turn. 'D' is 150 yards in advance of this turn, and will swing N. W. following wire as soon as M. G.'s on our front are disposed of. They have just had two killed trying to cross the path there. We are attacking what I believe is the left of their organized position.

"306th left flank platoon is at 97.0-75.1. This is *authentic*." (Their liaison officer had reported them a kilometer north of this point two days previous.)

" 'D' has been stopped. Patrols report large force 200 yards to N. M. G. fire from front and right. Rifle fire from N. apparently very close. Some fire from left."

Major M'Kinney had been placed in charge of operations on the front, and had determined upon a turning movement from the east; but an attack at early morning of the sixth, delivered on the right by "A," "B," and "D," and continued by steady pressure throughout the day, advanced the line there only slightly beyond the position held by "E" four days before, and did little more than move the field of operations to that point. At night "M" Company was brought up into the line, and a bombardment of the supposed machine-gun positions effected with Stokes mortars. At dawn of the seventh the attack was resumed, and by noon the enemy showed the first signs of withdrawal.

Moving along the ridge from the east, under a constant machine-gun fire, and cutting its way through the wire, the battalion at length

reached a position of vantage. "D" was left
to continue a holding fire upon this front, while
"B," led by Lieutenant Tillman and supported
by "A" and "M," moving northwest along the
lower slopes, outflanked the left, already partly withdrawn, of the enemy. They advanced
in single-file along a winding trail, an ineffective fire passing overhead. It was done almost
without loss; yet to those who knew him the
death there of Sergeant Watson, then in command of "M" Company, marked the advance
with loss enough. He had pushed out to locate
a machine-gun firing from the flank, and fell
shot through from shoulder to hip. They
crossed the stream into the Bois de la Buironne
and stumbled upon a bombing party operating
against the right of the surrounded force. It
consisted of only seven or eight men, and some
may have escaped, but most were killed where
they were met. A few rods farther, and, a little before dusk, they had reached the Binar-
ville-Apremont road and the right of that
dreary graveyard with its beleaguered surviv-
ors.

Such is the story of the relief of the Surrounded Battalion, of which very little has thus far been written, and that little not always with accuracy. Without the slightest wish to begin unprofitable controversy, when, in a publication given as the official history of the division, it is stated:

"Simultaneously . . . came the electrifying news that the 308th had penetrated the enemy's position and reached Major Whittlesey, relieving his battered, famished, but unbeaten command. Nightfall of the seventh saw our victorious soldiers occupying a front . . . along the road held by the 153rd Brigade, with the latter in liaison to its left with the beleaguered battalion of the 308th."

In common justice to his regiment, the present writer feels obliged to protest. The testimony of innumerable and competent witnesses indicates that the remaining elements of the 308th, while joining in the attacks on the left, did not reach, nor see, the surrounded force until, after its relief by the 307th, it had withdrawn from the ground it had so bravely defended; and that, again after that relief had been effected, patrols sent east by the relieving force in search of the 153rd Brigade returned reporting it to be nearly a kilometer away on the right, and that it did not propose extending to the left.

As to the story of the Surrounded Battalion itself, it belongs primarily to the 308th, and should be told by them. The relation between their advance and the attack of "L" and "H" Companies of the 307th on their right is very difficult to establish, but the latter appears to have reached conclusion before the former was begun. Testimony is widely at variance and memory uncertain as to the exact hour at which events took place, nor is there any help in studying the hours stated in orders, as these were very often not even received at the hours set in them for action. The most probable conclusion seems to be that the attacking companies of the 307th unconsciously aided in breaking the way for Major Whittlesey's advance, since "L" Company's turning movement swept clear for a time at least almost the whole west end of the ridge; but the total lack of coöperation, and indeed ignorance of each other's whereabouts or intention, between these two elements of the brigade must be regarded as the primary cause for the agony that followed to each. The companies of the 307th, organized as a thin skirmish line, reconnoitering an as yet unknown and strongly defended position, had ten minutes in which to prepare and launch an assault in force. Their orders stated that the 308th would attack simultaneously upon their left, which it did not do; while the 308th, advancing somewhat later, were told that both the 307th on their right and the French upon their left were also advancing to extend the flanks of the position they were directed to occupy, which at that time was not actually the intention of either.

The very costly attacks delivered upon the hill to the west of the railroad appear to have been ill-advised. It seemed to be perhaps the strongest point of the enemy position, and there may have been something of international rivalry involved. The French, more elastic in their advance and retreat, and less concerned in never losing a foot of ground than in husbanding their fearfully depleted man-power,

having already swept beyond Binarville, had
been repulsed at La Palette Pavillion, and had
withdrawn largely beyond the former town.
There may have been an intention to show
them what American troops could do. But
apart from the great strength of this position
on the west it did not actually command the
ground held by Major Whittlesey's battalion,
and was still held by the enemy during the
night after the relief, but without effectively
interfering with the relieving force. The first
company launched in attack upon this hill was
the same which had broken through the enemy
line on the ridge to the east two days previous,
almost reaching the later coveted grounds. Had
that ground been then designated as the objective of attack, the writer, who was in command of that company, is convinced that it
could have been reached; and had the attack
been coördinated with that of the 308th, a connection with their right flank could have been
maintained. Or again, later, had they been
informed as to where the surrounded force was
located, which was known to their superiors,
and had they been given any option in the mat-

ter, they would most certainly have elected to
repeat their former attack over somewhat the
same path. But they were merely directed to
assault to the west, and did so in the supposi-
tion that the battalion they sought was somewhere beyond the crest of the plateau before
them; and when their attack was finally
checked there was no one left who had taken
any leading part in, or apparently had any
knowledge of, their previous success. The eastern ground had undoubtedly been strengthened
in the interim, and yet, save for an attack by
a platoon and a half of "C" Company, it does
not seem to have been seriously tested again;
while success there both appeared more probable, and if gained would have proved vastly
more effective, than upon the west where so
much effort and bloodshed were expended. The
final success was gained by passing completely
around the eastern flank of the enemy position.

But to return to the story of the Surrounded
Battalion itself. It had advanced under orders to occupy the north slope of the valley
stretching east from the Moulin des Charlevaux, and, after some loss, had there taken po-

sition by nightfall of October 2nd. "K" Company of the 307th, under command of Captain Holderman, who had joined the regiment on September 22nd from the 40th Division, reached position on the right of this force at about dawn of October 3rd. The force consisted of Companies "A," "B," "C," "H" and "G" of the 308th Infantry, under command of Major Whittlesey and Captain McMurtry, and two platoons of the 306th Machine Gun Battalion under Lieutenant Peabody; the position extended for some four hundred yards along the lower slope of the ridge between the Moulin des Charlevaux and the Bois de la Buironne. "K" Company, advancing over the lower shoulder of the southern ridge at the end of night, ran the gauntlet of some machine-gun fire and suffered some slight loss before reaching the farther valley. The messengers sent back to report their arrival and coördinates to Captain Blagden returned to "K" Company with the news that the runner-posts were gone, and the way was closed by the enemy; the ration-parties, which they had been promised would follow them, failed to arrive; and within the hour of their arrival they realized that they faced siege and starvation.

They had had a cooked meal before starting forward, but carried with them not a greater average than a single day's ration each. With the marshy stream close behind them, their water was assured, but, except at night, only at the price of casualties. The duty of the commander of "K" was clear, and he placed himself under the orders of Major Whittlesey. These were for him to push back the enemy who were closing in on the rear. Recrossing the valley, "K" encountered a system of wire which they traversed, but only to find other wire beyond, and were themselves in some danger of being cut off from the rest of the battalion. They fought out a rear-guard action and regained their former position, where they formed the defensive right flank of the force. The first enemy attack was delivered on the evening of the third, the grenade throwers advancing above the cut bank along the road behind a barrage fire of trench-mortars while, covered by an enfilading machine-gun fire, riflemen attempted to close on the flanks. The attack was beaten off, but with inevitable loss.

There was not, either then or later, any massed infantry assault in the commonly accepted meaning of the term; the method of attack which had astonished the world in the early struggles with the British for the Channel Ports or with the French for Verdun seemed by now to have passed out of their repertoire. With the possible exception of the Marne in mid-July, it is safe to say that American troops have never been faced with such methods, though in this instance the ground was singularly well suited to it. An assaulting wave could well have been massed under cover above the cut-bank and hurled down the hillslope across a position which had no natural strength. Had the determination of the German attack then and later been in any way comparable to that of the American defense, only one outcome would have been possible; but although a few of the enemy were killed within fifteen or twenty yards of "K" Company's front not a member of the company at any time saw a bayonet fixed on a German rifle. Against the methods actually used by the enemy the battalion's position on the steep hillside had several advantages. They were completely defiladed from the front, and, it soon became evident, could not be reached by hostile artillery; the swamp in their rear, which might have been a danger, proved only a defense from rear attack; but against the constant fire of trench-mortars they had little or no protection.

On the fourth there were bombing attacks during the morning, and in the afternoon an American barrage fell squarely upon their position—the fire to which "L" and "G" listened, passing above their heads as they advanced to their first attack up the throat of the ravine to the southwest. Carrier-pigeons were loosed, and their presence with the battalion comes rather as a surprise, calling for a change in the range of these guns, and the incident was not repeated. Two days later, when another barrage was laid down, it moved across the swamp to their rear, and, jumping their position, struck again before their front with a precision that could not have been bettered.

By noon of the second day the last of the

food had been eaten and starvation began to weaken the strength, but not the spirit, of the defending force; fortunately, though there were two nights of rain, there was no severe cold, as on the few days previous to their advance, to further exhaust their resistance. Patrols were frequently sent out in an effort to get through the surrounding cordon, but only one man, Private Krotashinski of "K" Company, succeeded in reaching the American lines, and very many did not come back. Aeroplanes sometimes tried to drop food to them, though never successfully. The days brought little change. There was a more or less constant fire of trench-mortars and of sniping, bursts of machine-gun fire from the flanks, small bombing attacks from over the cut bank, and an attack in some force at evening. There was the steady drain of casualties; the wounded, though given every possible aid, died from lack of the care that it was not possible to give, from loss of blood, from exhaustion, or from gangrene, and, dying, still shared the shallow rifle-pits with the living. It was a nightmare time, brightened only by the courage of all to see it through, and by the steady background of sound beyond the ridge to southward where their comrades could be heard hammering and hammering upon the wall that lay between. In that anvil chorus from across the hills, the slower throbbing of American chauchats, like the bagpipes at Lucknow, could always be distinguished from the swift sound of the German machine-guns, and as it sounded fainter or louder brought its message of hope.

At least one act of chivalry by the Germans should be recorded in fairness to an enemy whose reputation for chivalry is not high. A single man of "K," creeping down through the bushes to fill his canteen at the water-hole, where the bullets were constantly splashing, was shot through the leg and disabled. There a bombing-party of the enemy later found him, dressed his wound with care, and offered him his choice of being carried back with them as a prisoner or left to be found by his friends. He chose the latter, and was known to the company as their best-bandaged casualty.

On October 7th an American soldier, captured on patrol, was sent in to Major Whittlesey with a written demand for surrender. The message was in English, on clean paper, and had been written on a typewriter, something which certainly could not have been produced by any American battalion on the line. It was courteous to the verge of being flowery, a point worth mentioning because the rumor spread among the men that it was very bloodthirsty in character. On the contrary it began by commending the messenger to the Major with the assurance that he had been captured through no fault of his own and had shown himself a brave soldier. It then went on to state that relief by their comrades was clearly impossible, that the crying of their wounded was distressing to hear, and that in the name of humanity they would do best to surrender. In the face of such courtesy one may venture to question the accuracy of the reported answer, more especially as there was no one to whom it might be addressed; actually no message at all was returned, and the American messenger was retained with the command. But there was discourtesy enough, and good American spirit enough, too, for that matter, in the remark of a private over the incident. He asked Captain McMurtry whether it were true that they had been called upon to surrender, and being told that it was, without asking what answer, if any, had been returned, he pushed back his helmet and exclaimed:

"Why, the sons——!"

It is safe to say that the attitude was typical of the whole command, as was that of another soldier who, lying near an officer's feet, received a wound from a hand-grenade in the face. He looked up rather dazedly to ask how badly he seemed to be hurt, and being told to go down the slope to be bandaged, answered cheerfully:

"All right, sir, but I'll be right back."

It was considered as something of an April fool joke that Captain McMurtry was going about, quite unconsciously, with the wooden handle of a German potato-masher sticking in his back. The preservation of such a spirit under such conditions speaks worlds for the men and for the officers to whom they looked for guidance, since courage is as contagious as fear.

The name of humanity, already disregarded by Major Whittlesey, received perhaps a ruder shock when the enemy, during the same afternoon, attacked with flame-throwers. Certain memories of Neuviller in June will always abide with those who probed the secrets of that unhappy village, and will stamp with detestation the use of that weapon. The present attack was of very small compass, only two Germans being seen with *flammen-werfers*, and both of them being killed; it is thought, though not with certainty, that one man of "K" was first killed by them. Later it was learned, with probable truth, from the German major commanding, who was met after the armistice by an American officer at Coblenz, that he was awaiting a large supply of *flammen-werfers* for his final attack upon the position. So much for the piteous crying of wounded, and the dictates of humanity.

The flanks of the battalion had at first been strengthened with machine-guns, but these, on the right flank at least, had been knocked out by trench-mortars and replaced with chauchat teams. Ammunition was very low, so that orders had been given to fire only at well-defined targets—and enormous handicap in that close brush-fighting. Yet the evening attack of October 7th, preceded by an intense machine-gun barrage, was beaten off as successfully as had been the others. And then, a little after, there was a burst of rifle-fire off in the woods to the right, of rifle-fire which they had not fired and which was not fired at them, and men looked at each other as they lay, weak with hunger, among their delirious wounded and their sun-scorched dead, and they questioned each other with the look. And then, through the gathering twilight, a company of American infantry moved in upon them.

That was the end. Not another shot was fired upon that well-fought ground, until two nights later some long-distance artillery threw in a few shells. Company "B" was the first to arrive, led in by Lieutenant Tillman, and closely followed by "A" and "M." The ground was quickly outposted to the front and flanks, but without encountering a single enemy; then the rations, such as they carried, were distributed. By morning not a German was to be found on the ridge south of the valley and the valley itself presented a scene like some hospital or rest-area, filled with ambulances, trucks and staff-cars. "K" Company, which had gone in with eighty-six men, was able to march out with forty-three, of whom very many were wounded, and a like proportion obtained for the whole battalion of six hundred. Had fresh troops been available the enemy on the ridge to southward, already almost surrounded, might by quick action have been themselves intercepted and captured; but the limit of endeavor had for the time been reached, and they were allowed during the night to draw out to the west.

While the losses to the Brigade during these six bloody days must have been beyond all proportion to those inflicted on the enemy, and while it seems probable that the German general retirement was here actually delayed in the hopes of capturing the surrounded force, rather than that the enemy were compelled by their advance to retire—yet there can be no question but that the indomitable spirit of this defense has added a chapter to the tradition of American arms which will survive. It is to tradition, no less than to purpose, that the soul of a nation must cling, and upon which it must build its life. The tactical or strategic results of the defense or capture of Cemetery Hill and the Peach Orchard have long since vanished into the limbo of the past; but the tradition of courage there bequeathed to the nation, alike by the men of Hancock and of Pickett, will not vanish. And so, in lesser degree, will the siege of the Surrounded Battalion remain to enrich the story of America's part in the Great War.

CHAPTER XI

GRAND PRÉ

THE general withdrawal of the enemy lines upon this front, forced first by the fall of Montfaucon to the east, and later by that of Fleville and Chatel Chehery, where their communications to the north had been cut, was now resumed with added speed. The right of the First Corps and beyond it the Fifth, forging farther and farther ahead through the open ground, was winning miles of .forest for the 77th Division, with, for the moment, little effort upon their part; and from the flank of this growing salient on the east the 82nd Division, freshly thrown into the line, struck west across the front of the 28th. Both armies were sweeping northward to the Kriemhilde Stellung, the next line of German defense along the open valley of the Aire, which represented in fact the enemy's most vital remaining artery of

east and west communication. The Aire itself, a stream some fifty feet across and six to
eight feet deep, promised something of a barrier to the division's progress, and the northern
bank was strongly held by the enemy; the
wooded heights beyond Grand Pré had been
converted into a fortress, and the Bois des
Loges lay beside them.

At daybreak of October 9th, now with a new
colonel (since Lieutenant-Colonel Houghton
had been evacuated sick and replaced by Colonel Sheldon) the regiment had pushed forward,
against a delaying fire of machine-guns and artillery, some five kilometers to the Bois de la
Taille northeast of Lancon, where, for the first
time in nearly three weeks, it had briefly
emerged from that never-ending forest into
open grass-lands. On the eleventh the advance
had been resumed past Grand Ham, and, skirting the valley of the Aisne, to Chevieres and
the Bois de Negremont. The twelfth found
the First and part of the Third Battalions on
the line, with outposts along the railroad, and
their supporting platoons, together with the
Second Battalion, behind the wooded ridge of

SUN-SCORCHED AND DUST-COVERED DÉBRIS

the Bois de Negremont. An attempt by a patrol of "D" Company to cross the river on the broken bridge at Chevieres had been repulsed with loss, nor had the other patrols along the banks discovered any fords; an attempt by the engineers to throw bridges across at night had also been driven off by artillery and machine-gun fire. The enemy's strength had been everywhere developed, and his weakness not yet found when, for the morning of the fifteenth, a general assault was ordered. On the right the 158rd Brigade had on the fourteenth effected the capture of St. Juvin, and it was not probable that the 154th had anything to gain by further delaying their attack upon Grand Pré.

Morning broke with a thick white mist clinging over the open meadows, and blotting out the town of Grand Pré beyond the river. At six-thirty the American artillery opened fire upon the wooded hills, and an hour later the First Battalion advanced to the attack—"C" and "D" from the southeast, "B" and "A" from the south. Despite the protecting fog, the first movement of troops into the open brought a sweeping fire of artillery from the heights to the north of the town, and of machine-guns from the high ground, from the town itself, and from the north bank of the river. The troops moved forward slowly and

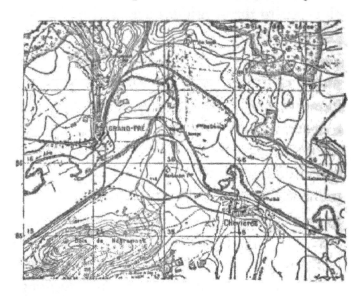

in little groups, using every feature of natural cover, and searching for targets for their fire. It was an open fire-fight, the first in which the regiment had ever engaged; and though the advantage of position and of cover lay entirely with the enemy, the relief from the blind struggling in the forest was enormous.

The Machine-Gun Company was helping with indirect fire from behind the ridge, and, for the first time, the one-pound cannon came most efficiently into action. By two P. M., under a constant storm from 77's, 88's, and machine-guns, which already had caused it casualties of an officer and sixteen men, "C" had built up its firing-line along the open south bank of the river. "D" held the narrow-gauge line behind it. "B," having also consumed the forenoon in its gradual advance, had carried its firing-line first to the tracks by the railroad station, and thence, by infiltration, to the trees and bushes of the river, where three platoons lined the bank on the left of the north and south roadway, while the fourth huddled down in support along the concrete platform of the railroad station. "A" held one platoon forward by the tracks and three along the north edge of the woods.

Enemy artillery-fire of H. E. and gas covered the whole area back to where the supporting battalions lay about La Noue le Coq, and where the lake by the ruined château was filled with the constant bubbling explosions of gas-shells. The machine-gun fire along the front never slackened. Captain Newcomb, who had joined the regiment a few days previous, was about noon put in command of the First Battalion, and, three hours later, Major M'Kinney was given general charge of the operations of the front. At eleven-thirty A. M. the Third Battalion had been pushed forward to the northeast for an attack on the right of "C" Company, and, though unable to reach the river, on account of the intensity of machine-gun fire from its farther bank, had got its two forward companies, "K" and "L," along the north apex of the railroad curve. "E" and "H" of the Second Battalion were, at two-thirty P. M., moved east across the open to Chevieres in an effort to connect with the 308th, which was advancing astride the river. Though the movement brought immediate shell-fire, the shallow depression in the ground along which they moved saved them from heavy casualties; but there also the north bank of the river was lined with machine-guns, preventing a further advance of either themselves or the 308th, still to the east. There they took position, under a

very constant fire, in a shallow trench bordering the road to Marcq. Their patrols discovered fords across the river northeast of Chevieres, but it was dark before "F" and "G"
were brought up to this ground and dug in by
Barbançon farm, covering the fords without
attempting to cross them.

In the meantime "B," extending its firing-
line to the west, had reached the sharp curve on
the river opposite the south end of the island,
and there, about five P. M., a possible ford was
found. Two earlier attempts to cross the river
elsewhere, by wading and by swimming, had
been driven back with heavy loss to the men in
the water; the first platoon had lost its lieutenant—crawling back two hundred yards under fire of snipers with a compound fracture of
the ankle—and all but eight of its men; the
ford just discovered by the fourth platoon was
held by an enemy outpost, and the man who
found it was shot while leading his platoon
to the place; four successive messengers sent
to this platoon from the Company P. C. at the
railroad station had been shot before reaching
it, but without deterring the fifth from going,

or from continuing to go. After dark a crossing at the ford was effected. The firing-line opened with everything it had against the west end of town, and under cover of this fire the troops continued to cross, "B," "A," "D," and "C," building up a new line beyond the river. As the supports came forward they carried planks from the railroad station, and footbridges were built from a fallen tree to a sandbank in the river, and across the canal beyond.

By two-thirty A. M. of the sixteenth almost the whole battalion had crossed to the island, and a patrol of "A" Company had crossed the canal and the wire to the edge of the town, where it was driven off with grenades by an enemy patrol, but without seemingly starting a general alarm. At three A. M. the last stage of the attack was begun.

"It was so dark you could see nothing and it had begun to rain. Yet this did not make us any more uncomfortable as practically all had either waded the river or fallen off the bridge in the darkness. I had fallen in three times. We started in single file across the canal and up a steep clay bank, cutting our way through a belt of low wire; I was standing on the bank, helping our heavily armed men on to an old road, and about half the column had gotten across, when a report sounded to our left. I had known that there was a Boche outpost somewhere there, and another about fifty yards away to the right of the bridge, but with the rain, and as absolute silence had been preserved, we had gotten by so far without being discovered. The report was that of a Very light, fired by some Boche who had probably heard a man fall into the canal. For a moment I thought it was all up, and aimed my pistol at the place, waiting; every man froze in his tracks. The light burst almost directly above the ford, glittered for a moment amidst the driving rain, and went out. Still silence, then a whispered word down the line, and we moved on. Just as the first gray streaks of dawn began to appear we started cleaning up the west end of the town."

"B" Company, which had so far borne the heaviest brunt of the attack, and with a loss of two officers and nearly forty men, was now placed as a covering party south of the town. "D" was sent to the west to ward off a possible counter-attack from that direction, one of its patrols there effecting the capture of an enemy outpost of four men and two light machine-guns, while another followed the Longwé road for nearly two kilometers without encountering resistance. "A" and "C," entering the town by a narrow alley in its western part, began the cleaning of it.

Formed as it was along a single street, organized principally for defense to the south, and taken completely by surprise, the cleaning up of the town was accomplished with astonishingly little loss. Not a shot had been fired since crossing the canal nor had any sentinel been met; in complete silence, and still almost in darkness, "C" turned to the east along the street, and "A" to the west. A single figure came round the corner of a building; there was a startled *"Mein Gott!"* and still in silence, with the muzzle of a pistol at his stomach, "A" Company had captured the first prisoner. He told of a garrison of one hundred and fifty in the town, all machine-gunners or automatic-riflemen, and led the way to the cellar occupied by the rest of his squad. At his summons they climbed out, their packs on their shoulders, and were passed along to the rear. There was some movement down the street, and a German officer passed, unconscious that American soldiers were flattened against the walls to right and left. He seemed to be leading out a relief of the guard, and all might have filed on into the ambush had not some one shouted "Hands up." The officer swung around, falling as he did so with a bullet through the neck; there followed a swift struggle in the half-light, and then a stampede back across the open fields to the north. Some were shot as they ran; a few were killed in the street, and some more made prisoners; but probably the greater part escaped. This completed the west end of the town, with twenty-three prisoners already on their way to the rear. "A" Company then turned east to help "C" in its more difficult task.

Here, as the surprise had been less complete, the resistance was much stronger; the fire of machine-guns and automatic rifles spouted from windows and cellars, and swept down the length of the street; fighting continued across the main square by the church till after nine A. M. Lieutenant Grubbs of "C" Company took a patrol around the backs of the buildings there to break this resistance, and seemingly succeeded, though he himself was not seen again. From here on the work was completed by three patrols of "A" Company, one of a lieutenant and six men clearing the buildings to the right of the street, another, similarly formed, clearing those to the left, while a sergeant and six men, recrossing the canal, went through the outbuildings to the east. Lieutenant Ross's patrol attempted also to clear the crest of the hill beyond the north edge of town, but were driven back by machine-gun fire; Lieutenant McCullough's, after reaching the last buildings to the northeast, were again driven back by grenades thrown from this same eminence; and Sergeant Swenson, occupying this last group of houses, though on the other side of the street, was effectually cut off from retreat.

The buildings occupied by this patrol formed the last group on the east of the road, and were separated by several rods from the continuous structures of the rest of the town. Although, during the unorganized resistance of the enemy, the patrol had drawn no fire while in the open meadows beyond the canal, hardly had they entered these buildings, about eleven A. M., when a messenger, crossing this open space toward them, was seen to fall; and a little later a messenger sent out by them was shot down on the same ground. The first was dead, but as the second, who had recklessly paused to thumb his nose at the hill-top, was still living, another went out to bring him in. He, too, was wounded, and the man he had sought to help died in his hands. The fire came both from a machine-gun seemingly just placed in position up the road to the north, and from the hill to the west of the road. The ground here rose in a sheer cliff above the roof-tops, from the upper ledge of which a machine-gun was fired and hand-grenades were thrown. Every effort of the patrol to return a sniping fire from the upper windows upon this position was driven off by grenades thrown through the roof, and a status quo was thus established lasting throughout the day.

Beyond this ledge of ground, and hidden by

it from sight, was a large château with formal gardens—the "citadel" which figures so largely in the subsequent story of the 78th Division upon this ground, and which has led to such unfortunate controversy as to which of the two divisions might fairly claim the taking of Grand Pré. Grand Pré, as a town, was undoubtedly taken, swept, and outposted throughout by the 307th Infantry; nor was there any reëntering of the town by the enemy during that day, as none passed the "A" Company patrol, which lay there awaiting relief until nightfall; nor when the patrol withdrew through the town did they see any sign of the enemy. But as a position the capture was not completed while the enemy still held this dominating keep; and perhaps one should add Bellejoyeuse Farm, a kilometer to the north, where his artillery seemed to be concentrated.

The relief by the 312th and 311th Infantries of the 78th Division began on the night of the fifteenth and sixteenth, and for the Second and Third Battalions of the 307th was completed by daybreak of the sixteenth. The Third Battalion had after dark been withdrawn from its position to the east of the town and returned to support, "L" Company outposting about the railroad station, and "I" endeavoring, though unsuccessfully, to effect liaison with the French on the left. The ground of the First Battalion was not taken over until one P. M.; and the farthest post, that of Sergeant Swenson's patrol, was never relieved at all. At about three P. M. the 812th withdrew from the northeast part of town; and at four an American barrage was put down on it, during which the outpost of "A" Company fortunately suffered no casualties. After that the enemy artillery took a hand, as they had been doing all over the town during much of the day, and at dusk the patrol withdrew, carrying its one wounded and leaving the two dead.

The taking of Grand Pré represents probably the most successful action of the regiment, for it is the only occasion on which it can fairly be said that the enemy were driven *en masse* from a position which they had fully intended to hold. Such occasions are much more rare than might be supposed, even in the course of a long, and eminently successful, advance. The war, as it was found by American troops, seems very seldom to have involved a fight to a finish on any one bit of ground; and the most that was usually accomplished was to hurry a withdrawal, for which the enemy were prepared at a later date. There were forty soldiers and an officer captured here, together with eight light and two heavy machine-guns. The ground afforded an opportunity which had long been lacking for the use of auxiliary arms; the Machine-Gun Company and the one-pound cannon platoon were able to bring an effective fire from the Bois de Negremont, over the heads of the troops, upon the houses of the town, and some of the accompanying guns could be laid "pointblank." The casualties of the regiment were returned as twenty-four killed, ninety-one wounded, seventeen missing, and seven gassed, one hundred and thirty-nine in all.

During the sixteenth and seventeenth the regiment was withdrawn to the Bois de la Taille, seven kilometers to the south, and thence on the next day as far to the southeast

as the Chêne Tondu. Here in an amphithea-
ter of ground on the eastern edge of the Bois
d'Apremont a collection of German huts and
barracks, ranged one above another on the
slope, gave lodging to the whole command,
and here for four days the regiment remained,
resting, bathing, and refitting. On the twenty-first it moved north six kilometers to a line
representing the Corps Line of Resistance, the
First Battalion near Fleville, the Second near
Cornay, and the Third near La Besonge, where
for four days they garrisoned and, which was
far more actual, dug the trenches. On the
twenty-fifth the battalions were again returned
to the Chêne Tondu, where they received replacements, five hundred for the regiment,
and remained in rest and training till the end
of the month.

CHAPTER XII

THE ADVANCE TO THE MEUSE

WHILE the 77th Division was making the most of its two weeks' respite from the line, the others, which had taken its place, were still hammering at the Kriemhilde Stellung—and progress had been very slow. The château and the high ground behind Grand Pré, Belle-joyeuse Farm, and the Bois des Loges had offered very stubborn resistance, so that when, on the last day of October, the division again resumed the front it was upon almost the same ground as that on which it had relinquished it. Yet, if little territory had been gained, many strong positions had been carried, and, for those that remained, not very much time was needed. The advance to the Meuse, although now officially listed as a part of the same offensive as that which had carried the division north, through the eighteen kilometers of the

242

Argonne Forest, was, at least from the division's standpoint, a new campaign.

For this advance the First Corps was formed, with the 77th Division in the center, the 80th upon its right, and the 78th on its left, the 153rd Brigade forming the front of the Division. On the morning of October 31st, the 307th Infantry was moved from its billets at Chêne Tondu six kilometers north to the vicinity of Pylone, a cluster of farms lying west of Cornay, and its orders were to follow, at about two kilometers, the rear elements of the 153rd Brigade. Throughout November 1st these did not advance, for the 153rd Brigade was attacking at Champigneulle the last organized line of enemy resistance south of the Meuse, and the resistance was still very strong. By morning of November 2nd this line had been broken, and the troops started forward on the long advance, an advance such as had never before during the war been opened to Allied troops, and which in five days should carry them, half famished and wholly exhausted, across thirty-eight kilometers of enemy territory to the river.

At dawn of the second, following the 306th Infantry, the Regiment advanced across the Aire, through St. Juvin, and on to a position east of the Moulin de Champigneulle. Champigneulle had been converted into a fortress, where trenches connected house to house, running across the village streets and through the cellars; but it was no longer a fortress nor a village, but a smouldering heap of ruins; the Allied artillery had stamped it out. In a single group to the east of the town lay eighty of the enemy's horses, killed by shell-fire. The regiment had dug in on their new position when after dark came orders for a further advance. The First Battalion was loaded on trucks, while the Second and Third took up the march. Verpel, where considerable resistance had been expected, and of which large-scale maps had been issued, showing every detail of the town and its defences—Verpel had been passed without a check; and, pushing north through the darkness, the trucks of the First Battalion reached Thenorgues. Here the whole country to the north was under water, and the 306th in the town reported that the line lay along the

·MAP·OF·
ARGONNE-
MEUSE·
·ADVANCE·OF·
·SEPT·26·TO·
·NOV·6·1918·

Scale of
kilometres

245

canal beyond it. Perhaps due to the rumble of motors in the street, or perhaps by chance, the enemy began a heavy shelling of the town, and the troops were withdrawn to the woods west of the Moulin de Thenorgues, where, after an advance of over ten kilometers, they took position with the other two battalions a little before dawn.

Toward noon of the same day, November 3rd, the advance was resumed, through Thenorgues and Buzancy, where the battered houses were still burning in the rain, and on through Bar eight kilometers north to Fontenoy. There had been intermittent shell-fire through the night and morning, which, as the cross-roads north of Harricourt were reached, grew to such intensity as to force a halt. And while they halted here, waiting for the shelling to cease, there passed overhead, like flocks of wild geese, squadron after squadron of aeroplanes, hundreds of allied planes, and the sky seemed black with them. They passed over to westward, and then from Authe came the continuous roar of their falling bombs. Whatever there was of enemy strength or munitions there marked for destruction, its destruction must have been very complete.

Here leaving the trail of the 305th, which, now in support, was heading northwest, the Regiment moved direct to Fontenoy, where was the Headquarters of the 306th on the line. Orders were received to take over the front at dawn, and about eleven P. M. the regiment again started forward. The roads were deep in mud and crowded with traffic; at St. Pierremont there was again shell-fire to be passed, and the town was partly afire; as almost always at night, it was raining. From the Headquarters of the forward battalion of the 306th, there established, little could be learned of the line; so, without guides, the First and Third Battalions moved forward behind skirmishers to the ridge southeast of Oches to await daylight. The Second Battalion remained in support west of St. Pierremont.

Dawn of November 4th revealed the advance elements of the 306th, which had not been found in the darkness, and an open ridge a mile to the northward pitted with machine-gun positions. The first forward movement of troops brought a sweeping fire from this position across the front, and from La Polka and Isly Farms to the east, where two enemy field-guns also went into action. There was no liaison with flanking organizations either to right or left. As the fire both from machine-guns and artillery was too intense to attempt a frontal assault across the intervening valley, the battalions clung to their positions along the crest, the Third on the right, near the highest point of the ridge, the First on the left, and the Second in close support under the reverse slope. Liaison patrols were sent out to the flanks, but not until nearly noon was the left of the 80th Division located on the Somman-the-St. Pierremont road, and, much later, the right of the 78th at Verrieres.

"A" Company, from the support of the First Battalion, moved down the western slope and up the valley into Oches, entering it about nine A. M.; but they were not the first of the Allies into the town. The old French interpreter, acting as Regimental Headquarters mess-officer, had been sent in with the mess-cart at an early hour, and was unsuspiciously in process of arranging a place for the head-quarters mess when he found that he shared the town with the Germans. There "A" Company discovered him in a highly conversational mood, and gathered that he was thinking much less of the glory of his position than of his dislike for American methods. The village was by this time free of the enemy, but fire sweeping down the valley from La Polka Farm and from the direction of La Berliere prevented any movement beyond it to the north. The accompanying guns were close behind, and a message to them brought a very prompt fire on the positions across the valley—a fire in which the Machine-Gun Company also joined. Here and there little figures were seen to jump up among the puffs of smoke and dust, and to hurry back over the open ridge. For the first time in their experience the chauchat-teams had visible targets at which to shoot.

The front line companies, "C," "D," "M," and "L," filtered a thin firing-line down the slope and across the valley bottom, but they could gain no ground up the farther slope. Flanking parties were sent along the saddleback toward La Polka and Isly, and artillery-fire was also directed on them, but there also very little ground was gained. The fire on both sides was extremely heavy; the crew of one of the American field-guns was wiped out by a direct hit, and in the course of the day the two leading battalions lost four officers and some sixty men; the Second Battalion, in support behind the hill, also suffered some losses from artillery fire, and its commanding officer, Major Prentice, was wounded by a long-distance machine-gun fire, curving down over the slope; there was heavy shelling of St. Pierremont to the rear. Again a vast flight of bombing-planes passed overhead to northward. Night brought no change beyond a closing up of the flanks by the 80th Division across the Rivau du Pré Billet and by the 308th Infantry into Oches.

At daybreak of November 5th, after a further shelling of the ridge opposite and of the La Polka position, the Regiment again started forward. Up till about five A. M. machine-gun fire had continued from the woods north of Oches, but to the Regiment's advance at six-thirty there was no further resistance on that ground. Pushing north against artillery fire, across country, and constantly urged to speed, the units began to lose cohesion. The wooded height of Mt. du Cygne was passed without a shot; most of the companies were swung northeast along the hog-back leading to Mt. Damion, while a part of "K" was detached to mop up La Berliere. A few civilians were found, but none of the enemy, who could now be seen drawing off across the open hills to the northwest. The Machine-Gun Company, which since leaving St. Pierremont had been carrying its guns by hand, and continued to do so without losing distance during the succeeding days, opened with effective fire on these targets. In front, on its commanding hill-crest, rose the town of Stonne, and toward this goal the advance continued with increasing speed. A platoon of "L," quite unconnected with the rest of the company, but accompanied by Colonel Sheldon, were the first troops to enter the town; they were closely followed in by "M," who, being lost from the battalion, were unaware that it, together with the First Battalion, was forming on Mt. Damion for an attack on the place. The Germans had left some five minutes before and two of them were captured in the streets.

The town was filthy with a litter of garbage and refuse strewn broadcast about it; and packed in the church and the graveyard was a crowd of civilians, gathered together for the hour of their deliverance. As the first American troops came down the street, close along the house-walls, in one tide of hysterical joy they streamed forth to greet them. Four years of bondage, in hatred and in fear, and these were their deliverers, a people whom they had never seen before, but had been taught to love, and the French do not try to conceal emotion. Old men, old women, and girls, their arms were around the necks of the soldiers, and their poor pillaged homes were ransacked for some token, some hidden treasure of food, to press, laughing and crying, into the hands of the hungry and tired men. It was worth much of hardship and of suffering to have been among the first troops into Stonne; not often is the fruit of victory spread at one's feet in such a harvest of human hearts.

As the First Battalion moved into the town an aeroplane swooped low over the housetops, dropping a message of congratulation, with news of American troops in La Besace to the east. Thither "K," "L," and "M" of the Third Battalion were sent, arriving about dark to find the place held by the 153rd Brigade Headquarters, with a battalion of troops. The enemy, still on the outskirts of town, were firing down the streets. "L" Company sent out a patrol of eight men, two from each platoon, under Lieutenant Hoover and Sergeant Cook, the latter already twice evacuated for wounds on other fronts, and who, as platoon leader, was not intended to have gone himself, only he said that his men were too tired to send. They had completed their route without loss, and had returned to the edge of town, when, for one fatal moment, they gathered at a crossroads in the darkness and driving rain; and a single shell, striking fairly in their midst, killed or wounded every man. Only one was able to walk back, badly wounded, to the company with the news that the sergeant and four others were killed, and the lieutenant mortally wounded.

Stonne too had been heavily shelled by the enemy, and a number of the civilians wounded, while others, their brief rejoicings over, moved out, pushing their scant belongings before them in wheel-barrows, into the night and the rain. The First Battalion pushed their outposts north through the woods to the line of the Huttes d'Ogny, with their main line along the Stonne-Warniforet road. The Second Battalion lay in support, some near the crucifix of Le Pain de Sucre, and some in the town. The night was one of drenching rain, of exhaustion, of hunger, and of some confusion, as the field messages of the Battalion Commanders indicate:

"My men are absolutely all in. Am trying to locate the front line of 308th. If you have this information it would be greatly appreciated."

"Third Battalion was in La Besace when your message reached me directing me not to occupy it. Rest of your message illegible from rain. 153rd Brigade Headquarters here and one battalion, 306th. I have put out cossack-posts along road west of town. Men very tired and have nothing to eat."

"6:15 A. M., November 6th.—No rations arrived as yet."

Yet, with or without rations, at six-thirty A. M. of November 6th, again the advance started, the First Battalion on the left, the Second on the right, and the Third in support. Pushing north through the Bois de Raucourt the two leading battalions were met, on the northern edge of the woods, by heavy machine-gun fire from Mongarni and Malmaison Farms, and, calling for artillery preparation, took position before them. This was delivered in upward of an hour's time, together with fire from the Machine-Gun Company; but the operation occupied the entire forenoon.

In the meantime, the Third Battalion, less "I" Company, which had become disconnected and joined to the First Battalion, started from La Besace with the colonel, supposedly in support, though not in touch with any other troops. A single mounted orderly sent forward as point, though quite unused to such work, most efficiently fulfilled his mission. There was a sudden burst of fire up the road, and the whole-hearted celerity of both horse and rider in their return gave the required warning of the enemy's presence. The battalion was deployed across the road about half-way between Haymoy Farm and the cross-roads to Flaba, "K" to the left of the road and "L" to the right; then the advance continued. "K" swung up over the high ground to the west, outflanking the positions of Mongarni and Malmaison, which were holding up the First and Second Battalions; "L" swept out the broken woods along the valley road; and "M" moved east through Flaba, the first troops into that town.

Standing on the open slope northeast of Ennemane Farm one could see the enemy streaming back over the bare hills to the westward, and south of them "K's" advancing skirmish line and artillery columns. It was a beautiful motion-picture of well-ordered war, but there was no contact between the two; the

Germans did not wait for that. Yet had it not been for a somewhat academic insistence upon artillery preparation of the ground south of Raucourt there might well have been contact. All troops were halted for upwards of an hour, while a total of seven shells was thrown at a supposed machine-gun position southwest of town, and while the enemy made good their escape.

A squad or two of "L" Company under Lieutenant Harkins were the first troops to enter Raucourt, closely followed in by "K," and the scenes of pathetic and hysterical joy at Stonne were everywhere repeated. Through the laughter and singing and tears one remembers the figure of an old man, with face gray and worn but alight with happiness, knocking down the German signs with a shovel. With scarcely a pause in the town, "K" pushed on down the valley to Haraucourt, the first troops to arrive, and were ordered still on to Beau Menil Farm. But by now the Third Battalion, still supposedly in support, was, as a unit, ceasing to exist; and the enthusiasm of mounted officers was overshooting the endurance of unfed men. The order was rescinded, and "K" went into bivouac at the road-forks west of Haraucourt.

"M," after stopping to mop up Flaba, though no enemy troops were found there, had joined "L" in the cabbage-field north of Ennemane Farm, and the two had made something of a meal of raw cabbage. With little prospect of anything more substantial they now went into bivouac at Nouveau Montjoie, two kilometers to the east of Raucourt, and a message from the battalion commander that evening states their grievance:

"My men, with exception of few who went through towns, have had nothing to eat to-day. with no prospect of anything to-morrow."

One platoon of "M," however, under Lieutenant Kisch, becoming separated from the rest, understanding their orders to be to press on to the northeast, and imagining themselves to be behind, had gone clear through to Villers-devant-Mouzon, which they reached at four-fifteen P. M., the first troops of the brigade to reach the Meuse. The Second Battalion went into bivouac at the eastern edge of the Bois du Chenois, while the First Battalion, passing through the Third at Haraucourt, took up the front of the advance through Angecourt and on to Remilly-sur-Meuse, reaching the river about four-thirty P. M. after an advance of eighteen kilometers.

During the last half of the way, although no resistance had been met, it was everywhere evident that the enemy had but just left. As the point of the advancing column entered Remilly a crashing explosion shook the town, telling that the enemy had blown up the bridge at their rear; Allicourt in flames to the northwest sent a flickering light through the dusk. Outposting the railroad tracks across Remilly and Petit Remilly, the First Battalion took up a defensive position on the heights east of Angecourt. Both flanks were open, for there was no liaison with other troops, and it is worth noting that the defense of the left flank, both on the line of resistance and of outposts, was entrusted to Captain Hubbell and his Machine-Gun Company. Still carrying their guns by hand, they had not only kept pace with this rapid and protracted advance, but it was Captain Hubbell's presence with the point of the advance which had saved it from being blown up with the bridge.

The region to the rear seemed to be filled with stray elements of troops from innumerable organizations, from the 1st, 6th, 42nd, and 80th Divisions, half-famished and exhausted men who had lost their regiments and their way; for in the latter stages of the desperately hurried advance straggling from all units had become serious, and the men, once separated, could find no information of their commands. A part of the 1st Division, either losing direction or traveling upon an independent schedule for Sedan, had crossed the sector of the 77th Division, and, in the darkness, had become engaged with part of the 42nd. Mounted generals and staff-officers, meeting platoons of infantry on the march, would order them upon new missions, of which their company or battalion commanders would never hear—nor for days thereafter would they hear of their platoons. Everywhere there was haste, exhaustion, and a growing disorganization.

That night, a sergeant from the 168th Infantry, 42nd Division, which previously had relieved the 78th, came up to effect liaison on the left, and reported the forward elements of his regiment to be on the hills west of Angecourt. The line was not closed up to the river until the following afternoon, when the 168th moved in on the left, and the Second Battalion of the 807th on the right, from Remilly to Villers-devant-Mouzon. On the afternoon of the seventh also the bridge across the canal at Allicourt was repaired, and an attempt made by the 302nd Engineers to build a bridge across the river at this point. A covering party from "B" Company, sent to aid in this operation, were soon engaged in a fight with enemy machine-guns on the farther shore; and, though the latter seemed at the end to be silenced, the Engineers had lost one man wounded, and the covering party from "B" one killed and seven wounded, and work on the bridge was discontinued.

There was shelling of Remilly throughout the day, with the pathetic killing of a few civilians—poor worn women, who had bravely endured four years of bondage and oppression, to die in the hour of their deliverance and at the very close of hostilities. There was a steady machine-gun duel across the river. Captain Hubbell had located eight enemy positions along the flats, and setting his own guns back in the interior of the houses, so that their flash and smoke were concealed, opened upon them through the windows; but they proved too deeply dug in to be reached. All day there was the sound of firing from the direction of Thelonne, in the sector of the 42nd, and once came a verbal request for flank assistance; but as the messenger insisted that the assistance was to be sent to the east, although he bore every evidence of having himself come from the west, and as the Second Battalion on the eastern flank knew of no such need, none was actually sent. No crossings were found of the river and there was no further infantry action.

Throughout the eighth, enemy shelling continued, concentrating on the cross-roads and towns, and mixed along the front with *minenwerfers*. There was little or no response, for, due to the condition of the roads and the rapidity of advance, the American guns had not yet caught up. On the night of the eighth the Second Battalion, increasing its front, took over that of the First Battalion, which withdrew to Haraucourt. On the ninth the 305th took over its right at Villers-devant-Mouzon, although, on account of the intensity of shellfire, the town itself could not be occupied; and on the same day the Third Battalion took over the right of the 167th Infantry at Thelonne, with the river front from Allicourt to the east of Pont Maugis. The latter relief was somewhat irregular in that the 167th left before the arrival on the ground of the Third Battalion.

We now come to that which, to the conscientious historian, is a most interesting and baffling controversy, namely the Bridges of the Meuse. The Regiment, or such part of it as is interested, may be classified under four heads, namely: those who believe in the bridges both at Allicourt and at Remilly; those who believe in the bridge at Allicourt but not in that at Remilly; those who believe in the bridge at Remilly but not in that at Allicourt; and those who believe in neither bridge. Each faction supports its conviction, for they cannot be called views, with incontrovertible proof, and freely impugns the enterprise, accuracy, and personal integrity of all other factions. The writer, never having looked upon the landscape in question, and therefore being quite impartial, has, after exhaustive research, arrived at no conclusion whatever. And yet the subject is significant, because it involves the passage of the Meuse, with the record of first over and farthest north, and such kindred matters, whose importance tends always to increase as the German machine-gun fades from an ever-present instrument of death to a picturesque topic of conversation. The reader is herewith offered both the facts and the fiction, and must make his own choice. He will do well, however, to bear in mind three modifying circumstances: first, that there was both a canal and a river, and that the former, though on the nearer side, was by some constantly, and by others invariably, referred to as the river; second, that the importance attached to a crossing of the river, somewhere and under any conditions, was quite out of proportion to any military consideration involved; and, third, that at an uncertain point in the interchange of reports the commanding officer of the First Battalion wrote:

"All former references in messages to 'Allicourt' should read 'Remilly.' "

To summarize then the reports: The 302nd Engineers report the bridge complete across canal and river at seven P. M., November 8th. At seven-forty P. M. Colonel Sheldon, in a message to the First Battalion, expresses a doubt that this has been accomplished and urges that a patrol of three be gotten across on a raft or by swimming. At eight P. M., November 9th, Company "B" writes:

"Footbridge over river is *reported* finished, and I *have* established a post of two chauchat-teams across river at 302.6-320.5."

And when the historian remonstrated that the coördinates given were those of a point across neither the river nor the canal, he was met by the ingenuous reply that they might be inexact, in that the sergeant who had provided them had at the time no map (and the civilian mind can scarcely realize the profound despair caused by such a statement). Yet it was said to be certain that the chauchat posts were es-

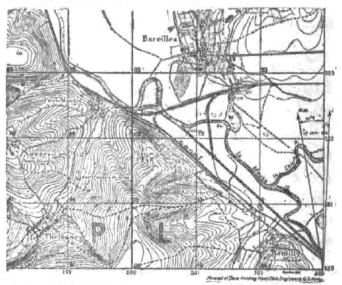

tablished across the river at Remilly by "B" Company, and that "F" Company had relieved these posts when taking over the sector—a fact flatly denied by "F" Company, who knew of no such posts. Also on November 9th "F" Company reports:

"Sergeant and six men of 'F' found footbridge at Remilly completed last night, and

266

sergeant crossed to northeast bank of Meuse at three A. M. Patrol of same sergeant and two men crossed bridge over Meuse at six-forty-five A. M. and went forward about one hundred meters unmolested, though there was distant fire on either flank."

At nine-fifty A. M. of November 10th the same officer of "F" Company reports as a novelty the discovery ₵of a footbridge at Remilly, and complains that "B" Company should not have warned him of its presence. He explains that the bridge on which the sergeant had crossed was actually at Allicourt. On the same day the commanding officer of the First Battalion reports:

"Lieutenant V. and one man tried to effect a crossing at Remilly, but were unable to cross river. He then worked north and crossed at Allicourt bridge, taking northeast direction to Douzy. He reports considerable traffic of trucks and wagons on road, but met no one. There is no bridge at Remilly."

Also on the tenth a Lieutenant H. reports:

"Left Remilly at twelve-fifteen P. M. with ten men and two scouts from Second Battalion

267

Headquarters, and went to 802.6-820.6"
(which is the exact place of crossing mentioned by "F" Company) "but found no bridge
there. I learned from the guide from 'F'
Company, who are in the town, that no bridge
has ever been there. There are the remains
of an old footbridge that looks as if it had been
destroyed long ago."

And he then describes following the river
north and crossing it at Allicourt.

At three-forty-five P. M. of the same day a
Lieutenant of "F" reports crossing with a sergeant and five men at Remilly, proceeding
northeast on unimproved Douzy road to 804.2-
821.4, hearing wagon traffic and meeting an
enemy patrol of seven or eight men coming
from Douzy, and stating in conclusion that a
covering party lay between the canal and the
river, which was recrossed at seven-thirty
P. M. On the eleventh another patrol of a
sergeant and five men, also from "F," is reported as crossing at Remilly and describing
the condition of the bridges over both river
and canal.

Finally, on November 11th, an officer of "L"

Company, which then held the Allicourt sector, reports:

"A private and myself patrolled the south bank of the Meuse in search of bridge from 302.1-321.3 to 301.4-322.1 and could find no bridge crossing the river. The sound of trucks traveling along road I discovered was water rushing over a mill-wheel at 301.4-321.9."

Also from the commanding officer of "L":

"I find that the bridge patrolled is not at 301.5-321.7, for there is no bridge there. There is evidence that a bridge had been attempted at that point, but no means of crossing the Meuse River effected. The bridge patrolled is across the canal."

And again:

"An officer with a corporal and two privates crossed the footbridge over canal, moving northeast to Meuse, at which point a footbridge once existed but which has been destroyed. Spans run out from both banks of river, leaving an opening of twenty-five to thirty feet in center. Swift current at this point."

And so the matter rests, but let us, at least for the sake of sentiment, conclude that the 807th Infantry patrolled across the Meuse.

Heavy shelling of the towns and cross-roads continued with projectiles varying from three to nine inches in caliber. The surgeon of the First Battalion had been killed while at work in the dressing station, and a single shell had wiped out the driver, five horses, and rolling-kitchen of the Machine-Gun Company. Yet in general the casualties were light. The American artillery, now in position, was replying, but not heavily, and with strangely restricted targets. First it was ordered that they should avoid firing upon the towns across the river, then that they should also avoid the cross-roads, then the cultivated fields; and finally came a strange and incredible rumor that an armistice was to be signed, and that all fire should cease.

Yet eleven A. M. of November 11th brought to that sector no sudden or dramatic silence of the four years' thunder of the guns—no outburst of rejoicing, nor any friendly greeting of old enemies. One might wish that it had, but it did not. There had been very little firing through the morning, and after eleven there was none. The ancient women, who had trundled out of town their wheelbarrows, loaded principally with nondescript bedding and still more ancient women, reappeared almost at once trundling them back again. And for the rest the troops, smoking the last of their tobacco, waited more hopefully, but quite inarticulately, for better rations. The first thrill of victory came on the twelfth, when a French battalion of Zouaves, in new uniforms, with colors flying and music playing, with the song of victory in their step and the light of it in their eyes, their officer flashing his sword in salute at their head, came swinging through the streets of Thelonne and Angecourt. It was the first glimpse any had had of the pomp and circumstance of war, and formed a delightful memory of its close.

CHAPTER XIII

THE HOME TRAIL

THE further story of the regiment may be briefly told; for, though the months seemed long in passing, they left behind them few milestones in memory to mark their progress. There were the long leagues of muddy road, back across the old battlefields and through the old ruins, and still on over a country untouched by war; till, in the first day of December, they reached a more or less permanent station near Chaumont. Clairvaux, Ville-sous-la-Ferté, La Ferté-sur-Aube, Jouvancourt, Dinteville, and Silvarouvres—the little villages stretched for a dozen kilometers along the valley of the Aube—a pleasant enough country when finally it had exhausted its capacity for rain, and the mud had frozen hard, and the steep pine-clad hills were covered with snow; but this was not until the last days of sojourn there. There

OLD BATTLEFIELDS AND RUINS

for five weeks they drilled, deloused, and equipped, but mostly drilled. To many it seemed that they drilled too much, for it was six hours a day and, on orders from high authority, "regardless of weather." Yet one who undertakes to disregard the weather of Northern France in winter is undertaking much, and it is more easily done in the office than in the mud. Then, too, the minds of all were filled with but one thought: "When are we going home?" The war was over, and it was an effort of mind that anything else should seem to matter.

An episode of interest to more than a few was the discovery of the loss, by almost all wounded officers, of all their baggage. This had been turned over through proper military channels, and then, as the old hymn has it, "not lost, but gone before"—that is, gone before the rightful owners could find it. It was squeezed dry by the friction of its passage through the above-mentioned channels, or else it grounded on a reef somewhere in mid-channel and never saw port at all. The writer found one bit of salvage from his bedding-roll washed up, as it were, in a bottle—a packet of papers marked with his name, and anonymously returned months afterward, which he had tenderly packed away, before entering the Argonne, in the center of the roll. Apart from this solitary Enoch Arden the bedding-roll foundered with all hands. His locker-trunk was returned from storage in the Government Storage Plant at Gievres, where it had been sent long before, with its lock torn off and a number of its crew washed overboard. Many officers received their suit-cases as empty derelicts with not a soul on board, but most received nothing, and cherished only a memory and a vanishing hope.

An episode of much more limited interest was the return of a certain company cook to cooking. He was an Italian, and though needing only a black patch over one eye and a wide-brimmed hat to pose successfully for the *Pirates of Penzance*, was yet a very excellent cook. Unfortunately he drank, and quite without sense of proportion; and, having so drunk, he would sharpen a carving-knife while he looked gloomily at the Mess Sergeant, whom he professed to dislike. The Mess Sergeant, while doing his duty to the very best of his ability, and ready in a general way to give his life for his country, took a growing aversion to the carving-knife, and complained about it to his captain. So the captain spoke quite sternly to the cook, explaining to him that he had failed to appreciate his many privileges, and had betrayed most of his trusts; finally, that he should make up his pack at once and report for duty on the outpost line. This had happened during July in Lorraine, and the captain had fervently hoped that contrition would soon follow, for the cook had to be substituted in the officers' mess by a man who was, properly speaking, a butcher. The cook, in spite of his rather moth-eaten piratical appearance, looked neither strong nor brave; and it seemed probable that a few nights of lonely sentry-post under sniping fire, or at most a few long marches with a pack, would prepare him again for his flesh-pots. But they didn't. He accepted his punishment meekly, in a combination of Italian and French, and then, having once tasted of the line, nothing would persuade him back to the kitchen.

When the picked platoon was chosen to represent the company in the proposed raid against
Ancerviller, though not chosen, since, among
other short-comings, he had almost never fired
a rifle nor drilled with a bayonet or grenade,
he none the less went. And so, till the end of
the war, he remained, and the company had
gained an excellent soldier, of whom there were
many, but had lost a superlative cook, of whom
there were no more.

Toward the middle of February came the
next stage of the long trail home, when the last
battalion of the regiment moved out at night,
under a cold half-moon, company after company in dim silhouette of packs and rifles, black
against the moonlit ice, with the calling of
good-byes behind, and twenty kilometers of
glare ice in front—that and a four-hour wait at
dawn for a train unheated, in numb and bitter
cold. The war was not over with the signing
of the armistice.

In the Embarkation Center about Le Mans
and Sablé life became pleasanter, for there the
spring was already beginning. Again there
were the wide-scattered billets—Asnieres,

Poillé, Fontenay, Avoise, Parcé, and La Rougealiere. There was continued drilling, but less of it, continued delousing, and more of it, equipping, some excellent baseball, and innumerable inspections, which quite definitely required a black and brilliant polish on shoes which were frankly intended to be rough and brown.

On February 24th the 77th Division was reviewed at Solesme by General Pershing. It had been reviewed at Florent just three months previously by General Alexander, but this latter occasion seemed more notable, and the Commander-in-Chief made a remarkable statement. So remarkable was it in fact that, for fear of misquotation, one almost hesitates to set it down. For he said:

"I consider the 77th Division one of the best—in fact it is, in my estimation, *the* best division in the A.E.F."

It is a distinction which, of course, every self-respecting division both claims and proves; but one can only assume the verdict of the Commander-in-Chief to be final. In any case it offered a most magnificent spectacle, massed upon the field in line of battalions formed in close column of companies, at one-half normal distance, showing with their steel helmets and fixed bayonets like some great Roman testudo or Macedonian phalanx of gleaming metal, a mighty and resistless engine of war. Yet, in the words of Canrobert: *"C'est magnifique, mais ce n'est pas la guerre."*

In March there was a military and athletic meet of all the divisions in the Embarkation Center, which the 77th Division won, and in which "H" Company of the 807th won both the platoon and company drill competition for all these divisions. Then on April 16th came the final move. It was full spring, and the meadows were jeweled with cowslips and violets, and the hedges were white with blackthorn—and, oh, how long ago and how untaught seemed the times in Upton, when the Regiment had adopted that emblem for its own —when the battalions moved out to their entraining points. At Avoise all the school children, with their teacher and village curé, lined the street to bid them good-bye, and every soldier came out with a flower in his cap or the

278

muzzle of his rifle. The teacher had written in English on his blackboard a message of affectionate farewell, and had taught each child to know it by heart. It is worth telling such things to those who have only heard of hostility between the Americans and the French.

The Regiment sailed from Brest between April 20th and 22nd, divided into its three battalions on board the *America*, the *Louisville*, and the *St. Louis*—the latter the same cruiser which had convoyed their eastward passage just a year and a day before—and by the first of May the last of them had reached New York. It was different, very different, from the going forth. There were excursion steamers in the Narrows, crowding on either side of the transports, covered with banners and placards of welcome, filled with brass bands and such fervently rejoicing people, shouting their quick, eager questions and greetings across the water. Then came the Statue of Liberty (which will always hereafter mean far more to her troops than ever she has meant before) and the strange, familiar pinnacles of the city—the docks of Hoboken and Long Island City, with

279

the American cobbles under foot—the eager, pressing throngs, crowded behind the iron bars, their reaching hands stretched through, and their eyes bright with tears and with worship. And the troops pressed forward along the narrow ways, their heads lifted as though for crowns, and the hot blood surging round their hearts, swallowing back their tears as they looked into those wonderful adoring faces—the roar of feet, the crashing thunder of the drums, the music echoing and reverberating through the streets, and the cheering, cheering, cheering till even the music was drowned into silence. How wonderful life seemed on that May-day evening to pilgrims coming back to it again— back from the already forgotten shadows of that twilight world beneath the portcullis of death. How the little troubles and purposes, that loom so large in the foreground of vision, how they dwindle and vanish down the long diminishing perspective of time; while higher and more and more commanding grows that great mountain of sorrow and of grandeur to which the pilgrimage has led, and to which the eyes of future generations in awe will turn.

280

THE HOME TRAIL

For the days through which we have lived have
been heroic days, and the world has not seen
their like before, nor will know them again;
and the memories of those days are a heritage
to the race of men which shall not be forgotten.
So the Regiment came back to Camp Upton,
where it was born, and was mustered out into
the citizenship from which it came.

FINIS

THE LAST ADVANCE

We have shed our blood with the English blood;
  We have bled with bleeding France;
We have joined our steel in the last appeal
  At the Red Tribunal of Chance,
Where shoulder to shoulder the nations stand
  For the glorious last advance.

Shoulder to shoulder, and heart to heart,
  Bound with a blood-red chain,
In the meadows where Fate has danced with Hate,
  In the drip of a blood-red rain—
In the trampled meadows where Death has reaped,
  Has sown, and has reaped again—
Brothers in pain and sick fatigue,
  And in purpose that recks not pain.

We have buried our dead on a thousand hills,
  And thousands unburied lie,
In battered village and shattered wood,
  Agape to the drenching sky,
Where they poured their blood in the trampled mud,
  As a witness to God on High—
As the last full price of sacrifice
  For that which shall never die.

THE LAST ADVANCE

But the ghosts of the twice-fought fields shall rise
　At the charging battalions' shout—
Shall whirl in the smoke of the last barrage
　Over bayonet-fight and rout—
Shall sing in the scream of passing shell
　As we sweep to the last redoubt.

For the hour has struck, and the kingdoms rock
　On the last red verge of war;
Our countless dead in the wind o'erhead
　At the final barrier—
One swift-drawn breath in the wind of Death,
　And the Merciful Gates before—
Where Freedom stands with outspread hands
　For ever and evermore.

　　　　．　．　．　．　．　．　．

And some shall come home through a sea of flags
　When the cannon their thunder cease;
And some shall lie alone with the sky
　In the valley of Long Release,
Where glorious dust is laid to dust,
　And rumors of war shall cease—
And the sunshine fair on their sepulcher
　Is the dawn of Eternal Peace.

W. K. R.

October, 1918
　Base Hospital No. 22, Beau Desert, France

APPENDIX

The Honor Roll of the 307th Infantry, which follows hereafter, is not quite complete, but it is the most nearly so now obtainable. Many of the Companies had lost all their records before the Armistice, and the casualty records at Washington are not as yet classified by organizations. In the published Divisional list, from which the one below is taken, the Company with which the writer served in October was given as having lost 44 killed or died of wounds, whereas the Company's own list showed 56. Wherever possible the Divisional list has been augmented, but this has been possible for only about half the Companies. The number of 56 above referred to is, according to available information, the largest in the Division, and is indeed very heavy, representing a total of 208 battle-casualties out of an original strength of 250 men. The names of wounded have not been included, since it was found impossible to compile such a list for more than a few of the Companies; neither, for most of the Companies, are the names of the men given who died of disease—where given they are marked (D.D.). The casualty figures obtained from Regimental Headquarters, of probable approximate accuracy, but having no list of corresponding names, were for the Regiment.

Missing	107
Killed	431
Wounded	1833
Total	2371

285

APPENDIX

In General March's official statement the 77th Division was placed ninth in the number of its losses, which were given as 2692 major casualties—or deaths from wounds, and wounds judged to be more or less permanently incapacitating for service. This is almost certainly an under-statement, and in the final parade of May 6th through New York the white banners about the catafalque of the Division bore approximately 2300 golden stars. The Division received 12,728 replacements of whom the Regiment received 1,628 enlisted men and 100 officers.

HONOR ROLL OF 307TH INFANTRY
COMPANY A

Both, Percy C.
Behrend, John.
Campbell, T. E., Sgt.
Caplo, Stanley.
Carlson, N. J.
Chambers, Ernest A.
Conay, Irving, Corp.
Curtis, Isaac W.
Dupois, Rene.
Formation, Carmine.
Fuller, T. L.
Goeres, Nick F.
Hamilton, Harley A.
Hart, M. L.
Haughian, Michael
Henion, W. H.
Jacobson, Roy D.
Kelley, J. B., Sgt.
Leonard, H. G., 1st Lt.

Liszewski, Antoni.
Logatto, Benjamin.
Mason, M. W., Corp.
Olson, Hans H.
Orth, Emanuel.
Owens, Joseph, Corp.
Pappalardi, Salvatore.
Rogers, Robert, Sgt.
Schumm, K. H., Sgt.
Seagriff, James H.
Specht, Walter.
Stanbitz, Philip.
Stuart, Ned.
Studlien, Eugene N.
Sullivan, Nile A.
Taylor, Henry T.
Wood, Francis E.
Ziszewski, Antoni.

APPENDIX

Company B

Bardman, B.
Baty, Christian A.
Blackburn, John.
Breth, Louis.
Brophy, W. F.
Burke, Frank W., Sgt.
Carlo, Michael.
Conner, James.
Cullen, Richard.
Dolan, John P.
Donkers, J. V.
Falliard, James, Jr.
Flanagan, R., Corp.
Friedman, Irving.
Hanley, J. P.

Hausner, Salie.
Kelly, John E., Corp.
Knab, Peter T.
Millsap, Earl.
Nickerson, Alfred W.
Peterson, Albert C.
Peterson, E. W.
Rhynard, John R., Corp.
Ribo, Raffele,
Robare, Albert J., Corp.
Robinson, James.
Russell, Geo. F., Sgt.
Sellers, Elmer O.
Straus, Joseph.
Zukasky, Paul.

Company C

Abramowitz, Harry.
Anderson, Oscar D.
Black, Guy, 2d Lt.
Brittain, Alton K.
Carpenter, Frank B., Corp.
Corbett, Frank H.
Daunce, William.
Galt, Alex.
Gill, G. E., 2d Lt.
Grove, W. L., Sgt.
Gulotte, Stephen L., Corp.
Hamilton, Douglas O.
Holz, F. H., Sgt.

Hickman, Virden S.
McCann, Henry P.
McMahon, William R.
Mundee, John D.
Murnane, John D.
O'Hern, Joseph F.
Olmstead, H. R.
Phahl, George R.
Remo, Frank.
Sands, Julius.
Schaubaum, Samuel.
Self, Francis E.
Staats, Frederick.
Stengel, Alfred.

APPENDIX

Subke, Harry C.
Swirsky, Isidore.
Symbol, A.

Winkler, Benton W.
Woodburn, James S.
Zielintski, Frank.

COMPANY D

Ames, James H., Sgt.
Bernado, Giuseppe.
Bertany, Joseph.
Blundell, John.
Campbell, Ernest J.
De Long, Herbert W.
Duffy, Edward J.
Eckhoff, Nils.
Elliott, Archie J., Sgt.
Goonan, Edw., Corp.
Haley, T. J.
Hartnett, William F., Corp.
Havens, Herbert L.
Howard, Walter.
Hyman, Louis.
Jones, Thomas A.

Kidder, Harvey.
Klaiber, Paul.
Muhling, William M., Corp.
Murphy, J. J.
O'Loughlin, Frank.
Phanco, Harry L.
Rechlin, J. J., Sgt.
Rosenwold, Anders.
Saxe, J. J.
Schurr, Ralph.
Schwenke, F. E., Corp.
Stender, John H.
Tanney, Albin.
Williams, John W.
Woody, W. M., 2d Lt.

COMPANY E

Arbuckle, Wyatt L.
Arpin, J.
Brown, L.
Churchman, Oscar D.
Cuddeback, M. A.
De Long, H.
Ennis, C.
Gerstein, L.
Goldstein, Julius, Sgt.

Grubbs, Lee.
Guthrie, Farrand R.
Heinzel, Frank.
Hyman, L.
Hang, G.
Kirk, Chas. F.
Lane, William J., Corp.
Levy, Jacob.
Lik, John, Moccasin.

288

APPENDIX

Mea, Cone A.
Miller, Wm.
Mooney, John J.
Murdock, Lindsay E.
Newsome, Fred W.
O'Brien, J. C., 1st Lt.
O'Neill, John T.
Pisano, Carmello
Quigg, J., Sgt.
Roth, Benjamin W.
Scudder, P. J., 1st Lt.
Segnit, John A.
Slatopolsky, Jack.
Smith, George A.
Smith, George W.
Standerman, C., Corp.
Steigelman, C.

Steiner, Albert C.
Stomers, C. D., Corp.
Stuessy, Andrew.
Urge, J. J., Sgt.
Walker, Edgar.
Weir, John S.

Benta, W. C., (D.D.)
Burger, W., Corp., (D.D.)
Daniels, A. G., (D.D.)
Forman, H., (D.D.)
Fortunato, U., (D.D.)
Harmon, F. P., (D.D.)
Hasler, W. C., Corp., (D.D.)
Manning, J., (D.D.)
Vanderbegaerde, J., (D.D.)

Company F

Alvord, J. M.
Amdur, C.
Bridgeworth, I. W., Corp.
Crowley, E. J., Sgt.
Davis, E. J.
Doyle, W. J.
Dunne, G. R., Sgt.
Haupt, F., Corp.
Heston, G. S.
Heutte, A.
Kerber, Jacob.
Love, J. A.
Morgan, H.

Powers, P. J.
Riker, Walter T.
Rubenstein, E.
Schmidlin, C., Corp.
Schreck, J., Sgt.
Sonnenberg, C. J.

Byme, C. A., Sgt., (D.D.)
Hamilton, A. E., (D.D.)
Herrickson, A., (D.D.)
Schneider, E., (D.D.)
Swanson, J., (D.D.)
Ungvarsky, W., (D.D.)

APPENDIX

COMPANY G

Brady, Hugh., Corp.
Braman, R. C.
Blanchard, N. A.
Bunce, Charles, Sgt.
Carlson, E. E.
Coleman, J. J.
Cook, James.
Dittner, Henry.
Funatelli, Achille.
Grandy, L.
Hamilton, D.
Hennessey, Martin F.
Jobe, J.
Kennedy, Robert G.
Klamka, John.
Kuratowski, S.
Kwiatowski, Stanley.
Kyewski, John.
Lord, W. B., Corp.

McConnell, J. W., 2d Lt.
Menisree, M.
Morriscoe, M. J.
O'Brien, T. J.
Peppard, Paul L., Corp.
Prat, Henry E.
Prince, C. P., Sgt.
Pusateri, F.
Ritter, Frank.
Schuster, Harry G.
Schuster, W. E., Sgt.
Vento, Andrew.
Williams, Tom R.

LaDucs, N., (D.D.)
McKinney, A., (D.D.)
Rebetarre, V., (D.D.)
Scott, L., (D.D.)

COMPANY H

Ammerman, J. B.
Ankelman, Rudolph.
Blyleven, Harry.
Caplo, S.
Christiansen, Conrad J.
Di Mele, G., Corp.
Downs, George T.
Dubinski, P., Corp.
Everett, H. C., Sgt.
Ezzo, T.

Fallowell, C. W.
Farrell, B.
Fickbohm, C. H., Corp.
Furstenan, Carl L.
Grant, E., Capt.
Guarino, A.
Guerra, Juan.
Hamel, Henry.
Johnson, J. H.
Kenney, J., Corp.

APPENDIX

Klimasswaki, Victor.
Konopko, Wincents.
Lanphean, Oliver M.
Lieneck, P. G., Corp.
McAllister, William.
McCallister, J., Corp.
Marini, Michael.
Miles, G. H., Corp.
Murray, C. F., 1st Lt.
Mabbruch, J.
Oscar, John.
Pawlik, J.
Pennachio, Mark.

Romanchuk, Stephen.
Rotgard, Isidor, Corp.
Seeger, Philip J., 2d Lt.
Sigafoos, F. W.
Smith, George E.
Stein, Israel.
Walasck, John.
Watkins, Charles E.

Kneble, E., (D.D.)
McEntarfer, J., (D.D.)
Price, J. J., (D.D.)

COMPANY I

Buttaglia, Salvatore.
Brennan, Edw. C., Corp.
Driscoll, William.
Falco, Thos. J., Corp.
Fallon, Wm. H., Corp.
Foley, James J., Corp.
Garland, Jack.
George, Henry.
Grimes, Patrick.
Hauser, George, Sgt.
Irwin, Wm. E., Jr.
Keane, John J.
Keating, Frank H.

Knopow, Charles.
Leberto, Giuseppe.
Maggio, James.
Olsen, H.
O'Neill, Patrick E.
Paddock, Allen W.
Rabinowitz, Wm. A.
Rook, William L.
Schaeffern, Jacob J.
Schindler, Jesse A.
Schmidt, Jacob D.
Talmas, J.
Terpilowsky, B.

COMPANY K

Ammon, Tobias.
Anderson, Gus.
Bang, John.

Blowers, Bert L.
Cafferty, Patrick J.
Church, R. G.

291

APPENDIX

Cole, Harvey R.
Crouse, William P.
Gotti, Albert J., Corp.
Hochman, Jacob, Sgt.
Johnson, Charley.
Klein, David.
Lekan, Mike.
Lipasti, Frank I.
Mahoney, James.
Malone, E. J.
Manfredi, John.
Nabbruck, John.
Neitizbie, J.

Palermo, Joseph.
Peiffer, W. E., Corp.
Pelkey, J.
Perry, Emil.
Rumsey, W. T.
Rust, Louis, Corp.
Seamolla, L.
Stall, W. H.
Swackhammer, George.
Szablinski, Wladslaw.
Tisnower, I., Corp.
Woodland, W. W.

Company L

Brodsky, Philys.
Brozholm, S. F. S.
Conti, Jos.
Cook, Percy E., Sgt.
Crabtree, Walter J., Corp.
Cuifetelli, L.
D'Elio, R.
Davenport, T. S.
Dinits, Sam.
Dreswicki, Raphael A.
Felter, Earle B., 1st Lt.
Florence, J.
Fuchs, Walter, Sgt.
Gaffney, J. J.
Gilligan, P.
Guillaume, Alonzo H.
Harkowitz, Louis.
Henderson, W. E.
Hill, Arthur A.

Houghtaling, H. W., Corp
Hubbard, H. L.
Jappe, August.
Jones, John W.
Kees, George D.
Knox, Robert G.
Kulseth, M. A.
Laib, Michael.
Leyendecker, T.
Lindeberg, A. R.
Lippe, Oscar P., Sgt.
Lynch, Hugh E.
Markowitz, Louis.
Moore, G. L.
Mowicki, Jos.
Oselins, Hjalmar J.,
Palsted, Axel T., Corp.
Pariser, Harry, Corp.
Patterson, Robert H.

Rabbitt, Michael J.
Schreider, Ludwig T.
Schlaffer, H. Sgt.
Schwencke, F. E., Corp.
Skogen, Edwin B.
Smith, Edwin.
Solberg, Reinert.
Sorbye, Oscar L.
Sorenson, S. A.
Stockham, John L.
Thompson, Jack.

Torregrossa, J. L., Corp.
Whitaker, I. B.
Wilcox, F. A., Corp.
Wilkes, James H.
Wilson, William M.

Larson, H., (D.D.)
LeViness, Jos. J., (D.D.)
Phenes, B., (D.D.)
Schmidt, (D.D.)

COMPANY M

Bolton, George T.
Brown, Peter.
Cahill, W. F., 1st Lt.
Comma, John.
Chamberlain, F. M.
Cunningham, A. J.
Dorscheid, Floyd F.
Eike, Hartvik B.
Evoy, John P.
Feit, Ray J.
Frascati, G.
Gallagher, Patrick J.
Garthright, J. R.
Harder, C. J.
Hohler, G. H.
Howard, Bernard A.
Kelly, Clark L.
Klein, Walter C.
Kobernat, James F.
Kucharsky, Adam.
Leahy, B. P., Sergt.

McDermott, T. J.
McDonald, James.
McNamee, Joseph.
O'Connell, Daniel.
O'Rourke, M. F.
Page, John.
Praffes, Nicholas, Bgl.
Raber, William, Corp.
Regan, Michael, Corp.
Riffard, L. A., Corp.
Russo, Salvator.
Stein, George E.
Sullivan, John.
Sutphen, William E.
Tymon, James.
Waters, Hunley, Sgt.
Watson, Rbt. E., Sgt.

Glor, Lester, (D.D.)
Smith, C. S., (D.D.)

APPENDIX

MACHINE GUN COMPANY

Clark, Herbert J.
Freedman, Isaac N., Sgt.
Hershman, M. M., Sgt.
Munson, Eugene.
Nichols, R. L.

O'Connor, M. B.
Ray, Thomas J.
Warren, Casimir M.
Wentworth, William H.

HEADQUARTERS COMPANY

Blauvelt, Charles R.
Clinton, H. T., Corp.
Rice, F. D.

Riley, Joseph.
Smith, Lee S.

SUPPLY COMPANY

Scott, F. A., Capt.

SANITARY DETACHMENT

Alvey, Martin N.
Cieslinski, J. T., Sgt.
Hollander, Viel.
Kirsch, Louis.
Ohlson, Alfred H.

Rosenblum, I.
Schroeder, Hans C.
Sweeney, William J.
Walsh, Christopher T.
Wolf, Joseph, Jr.

OFFICERS WHO HAVE COMMANDED THE UNITS OF THE REGIMENTS

The following list has been given by the units concerned as that of the officers who have at any time been in command of them. The list is not meant to contain mere technicalities, as when an officer has been left briefly in command of a unit during the temporary occupation elsewhere of its actual commander. The names are given with the grade held during the period

APPENDIX

of command, and not that to which the officers may later have been promoted. Where an officer served in command of various units the notation of "wounded" after his name indicates that he was wounded while in command of that unit.

307TH INFANTRY

Colonel I. Erwin.
Lt.-Colonel R. A. Smith.
Lt.-Colonel J. A. Benjamin.
Lt.-Colonel E. A. Houghton (evac. sick).

Colonel R. Sheldon.
Colonel J. R. Hanney.
Lt.-Colonel W. H. Meyers.

FIRST BATTALION

Major P. P. Gardiner.
Captain C. Blagden.

Captain E. B. Newcomb.
Major J. F. M'Kinney.

COMPANY A

Captain C. Blagden (wounded).
Lieutenant J. W. Vardeman (injured).

Captain W. Harrigan (wounded).
Lieutenant N. W. Kenyon (killed).
Lieutenant J. McCearley.

COMPANY B

Captain B. Barrett (killed).
Lieutenant E. A. Butterfield (injured).
Lieutenant F. A. Tillman.

Lieutenant H. R. Weiman.
Captain L. O. Slagle.
Captain W. G. Green.
Lieutenant K. C. Lincoln.
Captain W. Jenkins.

Printed in the USA
CPSIA information can be obtained
at www.ICGtesting.com
LVHW051736121023
760950LV00005B/174

9 781019 433362